Pittsburgh Pirates 2019

A Baseball Companion

Edited by Patrick Dubuque, Aaron Gleeman and Bret Sayre

Baseball Prospectus

Craig Brown and Dave Pease, Consultant Editors
Rob McQuown and Harry Pavlidis, Statistics Editors

Copyright © 2019 by DIY Baseball, LLC.
All rights reserved

This book or any part thereof may not be reproduced or transmitted in any form or by any means, electronic or mechanical, including photocopying, recording, or by any information storage and retrieval system, without permission in writing from the publisher.

Limit of Liability/Disclaimer of Warranty: While the publisher and the author have used their best efforts in preparing this book, they make no representations or warranties with respect to the accuracy or completeness of the contents of this book and specifically disclaim any implied warranties of merchantability or fitness for a particular purpose. No warranty may be created or extended by sales representatives or written sales materials. The advice and strategies contained herein may not be suitable for your situation. You should consult with a professional where appropriate. Neither the publisher nor the author shall be liable for any loss of profit or any other commercial damages, including but not limited to special, incidental, consequential, or other damages.

Library of Congress Cataloging-in-Publication Data:
paperback
ISBN-13: 978-1-949332-50-6

Project Credits
Cover Design: Kathleen Dyson
Interior Design and Production: Jeff Pease, Dave Pease
Layout: Jeff Pease, Dave Pease

Baseball icon courtesy of Uberux, from https://www.shareicon.net/author/uberux

Ballpark diagram courtesy of Lou Spirito/THIRTY81 Project, https://thirty81project.com/

Manufactured in the United States of America
10 9 8 7 6 5 4 3 2 1

Table of Contents

Foreword v
    Rob Mains

Statistical Introduction vii

Part 1: Team Analysis

Table for Two: Previewing the 2019 Pittsburgh Pirates 3
    Rob Mains and Matthew Trueblood

Performance Graphs 9

2018 Team Performance 10

2019 Team Projections 11

Team Personnel 12

PNC Park Stats 13

Pirates Team Analysis 15

Part 2: Player Analysis

Pirates Player Analysis 22

Pirates Prospects 103

Part 3: Featured Articles

The Hole in The Shift is Fixing Itself 117
    Russell Carleton

The State of the Quality Start 121
    Rob Mains

Heads-Up Hacking—The First Pitch 127
    Matthew Trueblood

A Hymn for the Index Stat 133
    Patrick Dubuque

Index of Names 137

Foreword

Rob Mains

Welcome to this companion of the 2019 Pittsburgh Pirates. We at Baseball Prospectus are excited to provide this analysis of the Pirates.

Our website, Baseball Prospectus, is a leader in delivering high-quality commentary and data to baseball fans everywhere. To some, those words—commentary and data—appear mutually exclusive. There are people out there who believe that traditional analysis and advanced analytics must run on different paths. But the simplistic narrative of stats vs. traditionalists just isn't true. Every team's analytics department interacts with scouting, development, and major league operations with a common goal: Delivering a championship. New technologies, like radar tracking of pitch speeds and movement, enable talent evaluators to focus on qualitative aspects of pitching like mechanics and pitch sequencing. In-game strategies like infield shifts, based on batters' hit tendencies, help turn balls in play into outs. Hitters use information to adjust their swings to maximize run production.

All these numbers can seem, at best, intimidating, and at worst, counterproductive to the casual fan. Even as technology and analysis have embedded themselves deeply into the way teams run, it can often feel like statistics create a displacement between the viewer and the sport, breaking them out of the action. And yet every fan incorporates the numbers to some degree; stats like batting average and earned run average, so fundamental to how we talk about performance, are actually complicated formulas. They don't bother people because those formulas have become second nature, as easy to translate as the action on the field.

Along the way, new statistics have entered baseball's lexicon. You'll see some of them, like on-base percentage (which measures a batter's ability to get on base via walk, hit batter, or hit), OPS (on-base plus slugging), and average exit velocity (the speed of balls off a hitter's bat) on broadcasts. Others, like DRC+, might well be new to you. Some of them have been well-defined to the public, others haven't. That lack of context has created ambiguity. Fans know that a ball hit 100 mph is scorched, but does that mean extra bases? (Not if it's hit on the ground or high in the air it doesn't.)

For those who are amenable to them, the new statistics can increase the enjoyment and understanding of the game. They can help fans identify when a pitcher is tiring, when a stolen base or a bunt attempt makes sense (and, more often, when it doesn't), or how a team's lineup might be constructed. Websites like Baseball Prospectus add to that understanding by weaving metrics into the narrative of the game. That's the goal of this publication: to take some of the newer, more complicated statistics and make them as intuitive as the ones on the back of old baseball cards.

But you don't need to love analytics to love baseball. The fans at BP who worked together to write this guide are captivated first and foremost by the game itself. We're drawn to Aaron Judge's power, Francisco Lindor's glove, Billy Hamilton's speed and Patrick Corbin's slider and don't need numbers to tell us why they're so mesmerizing. The underlying statistics provide depth to the game that we all love.

We hope you'll find that this guide helps you better understand the Pirates. Our analysts have studied the team's major league personnel and its minor league affiliates to identify their strengths and weaknesses, both the obvious ones and those that only a careful dissection of players' performances—yes, including the data—can reveal. You don't need us to tell you who was good and who wasn't in 2018, but our models and writers can help you project how each player is going to perform this year and beyond, and appreciate the greatness of each new game as it unfolds. As in the sport itself, the human and analytic components combine to generate a deeper overall understanding.

Think back to the first time you saw a baseball game on a high-definition TV. You'd grown familiar with how the game looked and felt on a picture tube. But new TV allowed you to see details that you'd never seen before. That's how advanced statistics work. The game itself is why you're here and why you're buying this. (And, for that matter, why we wrote it.) The statistical measures provide the sharper focus, the detail, the depth of knowledge that you didn't have before, generating an overall superior picture. Enjoy the view.

—Rob Mains is an author of Baseball Prospectus.

Statistical Introduction

Sports are, fundamentally, a blend of athletic endeavor and storytelling. Baseball, like any other sport, tells its stories in so many ways: in the arc of a game from the stands or a season from the box scores, in photos, or even in numbers. At Baseball Prospectus, we understand that statistics don't replace observation or any of baseball's stories, but complement everything else that makes the game so much fun.

What stats help us with is with patterns and precision, variance and value. This book can help you learn things you may not see from watching a game or hundred, whether it's the path of a career over time or the breadth of the entire MLB. We'd also never ask you to choose between our numbers and the experience of viewing a game from the cheap seats or the comfort of your home; our publication combines running the numbers with observations and wisdom from some of the brightest minds we can find. But if you *do* want to learn more about the numbers beyond what's on the backs of player jerseys, let us help explain.

Offense

At the end of this past year, we've revised our methodology for determining batting value. Long-time readers of Baseball Prospectus will notice that we've retired True Average in favor of a new metric: Deserved Runs Created Plus (DRC+). Developed by Jonathan Judge and our stats team, this statistic measures everything a player does at the plate–reaching base, hitting for power, making outs, and moving runners over–and puts it on a scale where 100 equals league-average performance. A DRC+ of 150 is terrific, a DRC+ of 100 is average, and a DRC+ of 75 means you better be an excellent defender.

DRC+ also does a better job than any of our previous metrics in taking contextual factors into account. The model adjusts for how the park affects performance, but also for things like the talent of the opposing pitcher, value of different types of batted-ball events, league, temperature, and other factors. It's able to describe a player's expected offensive contribution than any other statistic we've found over the years, and also does a better job of predicting future performance as well.

The other aspect of run-scoring is baserunning, which we quantify using Baserunning Runs. BRR not only records the value of stolen bases (or getting caught in the act), but also accounts for a runner's ability to go first to third on a single or advance on a fly ball.

Defense

Where offensive value is *relatively* easy to identify and understand, defensive value is ... not. Over the past dozen years, the sabermetric community has focused mostly on stats based on zone data: a real-live human person records the type of batted ball and estimated landing location, and models are created that give expected outs. From there, you can compare fielders' actual outs to those expected ones. Simple, right?

Unfortunately, zone data has two major issues. First, zone data is recorded by commercial data providers who keep the raw data private unless you pay for it. (All the statistics we build in this book and on our website use public data as inputs.) That hurts our ability to test assumptions or duplicate results. Second, over the years it has become apparent that there's quite a bit of "noise" in zone-based fielding analysis. Sometimes the conclusions drawn from zone data don't hold up to scrutiny, and sometimes the different data provided by different providers don't look anything alike, giving wildly different results. Sometimes the hard-working professional stringers or scorers might unknowingly inflict unconscious bias into the mix: for example good fielders will often be credited with more expected outs despite the data, and ballparks with high press boxes tend to score more line drives than ones with a lower press box.

Enter our Fielding Runs Above Average (FRAA). For most positions, FRAA is built from play-by-play data, which allows us to avoid the subjectivity found in many other fielding metrics. The idea is this: count how many fielding plays are made by a given player and compare that to expected plays for an average fielder at their position (based on pitcher ground-ball tendencies and batter handedness). Then we adjust for park and base-out situations.

When it comes to catchers, our methodology is a little different thanks to the laundry list of responsibilities they're tasked with beyond just, well, catching and throwing the ball. By now you've probably heard about "framing" or the art of making umpires more likely to call balls outside the strike zone for strikes. To put this into one tidy number, we incorporate pitch tracking data (for the years it exists) and adjust for important factors like pitcher, umpire, batter, and home-field advantage using a mixed-model approach. This grants us a number for how many strikes the catcher is personally adding to (or subtracting from) his pitchers' performance ... which we then convert to runs added or lost using linear weights.

Framing is one of the biggest parts of determining catcher value, but we also take into account blocking balls from going past, whether a scorer deems it a passed ball or a wild pitch. We use a similar approach–one that really benefits from the pitch tracking data that tells us what ends up in the dirt and what doesn't. We also include a catcher's ability to prevent stolen bases and how well they field balls in play, and *finally* we come up with our FRAA for catchers.

Pitching

Both pitching and fielding make up the half of baseball that isn't run scoring: run prevention. Separating pitching from fielding is a tough task, and most recent pitching analysis has branched off from Voros McCracken's famous (and controversial) statement, "There is little if any difference among major-league pitchers in their ability to prevent hits on balls hit in the field of play." The research of the analytic community has validated this to some extent, and there are a host of "defense-independent" pitching measures that have been developed to try and extricate the effect of the defense behind a hurler from the pitcher's work.

Our solution to this quandry is Deserved Run Average (DRA), our core pitching metric. DRA looks like earned run average (ERA), the tried-and-true pitching stat you've seen on every baseball broadcast or box score from the past century, but it's very different. To start, DRA takes an event-by-event look at what the pitchers does, and adjusts the value of that event based on different environmental factors like park, batter, catcher, umpire, base-out situation, run differential, inning, defense, home field advantage, pitcher role, and temperature. That mixed model gives us a pitcher's expected contribution, similar to what we do for our DRC+ model for hitters and FRAA model for catchers. (Oh, and we also consider the pitcher's effect on basestealing and on balls getting past the catcher.)

It's important to note that DRA is set to the scale of runs allowed per nine innings (RA9) instead of ERA, which makes DRA's scale slightly higher than ERA's. The reason for this is because ERA tends to overrate three types of pitchers:

1. Pitchers who play in parks where scorers hand out more errors. Official scorers differ significantly in the frequency at which they assign errors to fielders.
2. Ground-ball pitchers, because a substantial proportion of errors occur on grounders.
3. Pitchers who aren't very good. Better pitchers often allow fewer unearned runs than bad pitchers, because good pitchers tend to find ways to get out of jams.

Pittsburgh Pirates 2019

Since the last time you picked up an edition of this book, we've also made a few minor changes to DRA to make it better. Recent research into "tunneling"–the act of throwing consecutive pitches that appear similar from a batter's point of view until after the swing decision point–data has given us a new contextual factor to account for in DRA: plate distance. This refers to the distance between successive pitches as they approach the plate, and while it has a smaller effect than factors like velocity or whiff rate, it still can help explain pitcher strikeout rate in our model.

New Pitching Metrics for 2019

We're including a few "new" pitching metrics for 2019's suite of Baseball Prospectus publications, but you may be familiar with them if you've spent time scouring the internet for stats.

Fastball Percentage

Our fastball percentage (FB%) statistic measures how frequently a pitcher throws a pitch classified as a "fastball," measured as a percentage of overall pitches thrown. We qualify three types of fastballs:

1. The traditional four-seam fastball;
2. The two-seam fastball or sinker;
3. "Hard cutters," which are pitches that have the movement profile of a cut fastball and are used as the pitcher's primary offering or in place of a more traditional fastball.

For example, a pitcher with a FB% of 67 throws any combination of these three pitches about two-thirds of the time.

Whiff Rate

Everybody loves a swing and a miss, and whiff rate (WHF) measures how frequently pitchers induce a swinging strike. To calculate WHF, we add up all the pitches thrown that ended with a swinging strike, then divide that number by a pitcher's total pitches thrown. Most often, high whiff rates correlate with high strikeout rates (and overall effective pitcher performance).

Called Strike Probability

Called Strike Probability (CSP) is a number that represents the likelihood that all of a pitcher's pitches will be called a strike while controlling for location, pitcher and batter handedness, umpire and count. Here's how it works: on each pitch, our model determines how many times (out of 100) that a similar pitch was called for a strike given those factors mentioned above, and when normalized for each batter's strike zone. Then we average the CSP for all pitches thrown by a pitcher in a season, and that gives us the yearly CSP percentage you see in the stats boxes.

As you might imagine, pitchers with a higher CSP are more likely to work in the zone, where pitchers with a lower CSP are likely locating their pitches outside the normal strike zone, for better or for worse.

Projections

Many of you aren't turning to this book just for a look at what a player has done, but for a look at what a player is going to do: the PECOTA projections. PECOTA, initially developed by Nate Silver (who has moved on to greater fame as a political analyst), consists of three parts:

1. Major-league equivalencies, which use minor-league statistics to project how a player will perform in the major leagues;
2. Baseline forecasts, which use weighted averages and regression to the mean to estimate a player's current true talent level; and
3. Aging curves, which uses the career paths of comparable players to estimate how a player's statistics are likely to change over time.

With all those important things covered, let's take a look at what's in the book this year.

Team Prospectus

You bought this book to learn more about your favorite (or maybe least-favorite, who are we to judge?) team, so let's talk about them. After a thoughtful preview of the 2019 season, you'll be presented with our Team Prospectus. This outlines many of the key statistics for each team's 2018 season, as well as a very inviting stadium diagram.

First you'll find the Performance Graphs page. The first is the 2018 Hit List Ranking. This shows our Hit List Rank for the team on each day of the 2018 season and is intended to give you a picture of the ups and downs of the team's season, including their highest and lowest ranks of the year. Hit List Rank measures overall team performance and drives the Hit List Power Rankings at the baseballprospectus.com website.

The second graph is Committed Payroll and helps you see how the team's payroll has compared to the MLB and divisional average payrolls over time. Payroll figures are currents as of January 1, 2019; with so many free agents still unsigned as of this writing, the final 2018 figure will likely be significantly different for many teams. (In the meantime, you can always find the most current data at Baseball Prospectus' Cot's Baseball Contracts page.)

Pittsburgh Pirates 2019

The third graph is Farm System Ranking and displays how the Baseball Prospectus prospect team has ranked the organization's farm system since 2007. It also indicates the highest and lowest ranks that the farm system achieved over that time.

We start the Team Performance page with the squad's unadjusted and third-order 2018 win-loss records, presented in divisional context. We then list the three highest performing hitters and pitchers by WARP for 2018. Beneath that are a host of other team statistics. **Pythag** presents an adjusted 2018 winning percentage, calculated by taking runs scored per game (**RS/G**) and runs allowed per game (**RA/G**) for the team, and running them through a version of Bill James' Pythagorean formula that was refined and improved by David Smyth and Brandon Heipp. (The formula is called "Pythagenpat," which is equally fun to type and to say.)

Next up is **DRC+**, described earlier, to indicate the overall hitting ability of the team either above or below league-average. Run prevention on the pitching side is covered by **DRA** (also mentioned earlier) and another metric: Fielding Independent Pitching (**FIP**), which calculates another ERA-like statistic based on strikeouts, walks, and home runs recorded. Defensive Efficiency Rating (**DER**) tells us the percentage of balls in play turned into outs for the team, and is a quick fielding shorthand that rounds out run prevention.

After that, we have several measures related to roster composition, as opposed to on-field performance. **B-Age** and **P-Age** tell us the average age of a team's batters and pitchers, respectively. **Salary** is the combined team payroll for all on-field players, and Doug Pappas' Marginal Dollars per Marginal Win (**M$/MW**) tells us how much money a team spent to earn production above replacement level.

Ending this batch of statistics is the number of disabled list days a team had over the season (**DL Days**) and the amount of salary paid to players on the disabled list (**$ on DL**); this final number is expressed as a percentage of total payroll.

Next to each of these stats, we've listed each team's MLB rank in that category from 1st to 30th. In this, 1st always indicates a positive outcome and 30th a negative outcome, except in the case of salary–1st is highest.

The Team Projections page is intended to convey the team's operational capacity entering the 2019 season. We start with the team's PECOTA projected record for 2019, again in divisional context. The **+/-** column indicates how many more or less wins the team is projected to get than they got in 2018. We then list the three highest projected hitters and pitchers by WARP for 2018. A brief farm system summary follows, with the team's top prospect and number of BP Top 101 Prospects. Finally, we list the key new players and departed players, along with their 2019 projected WARP.

Alex Bregman 3B

Born: 03/30/94 Age: 25 Bats: R Throws: R
Height: 6'0" Weight: 180 Origin: Round 1, 2015 Draft (#2 overall)

YEAR	TEAM	LVL	AGE	PA	R	2B	3B	HR	RBI	BB	K	SB	CS	AVG/OBP/SLG
2016	CCH	AA	22	285	54	16	2	14	46	42	26	5	3	.297/.415/.559
2016	FRE	AAA	22	83	17	6	0	6	15	5	12	2	1	.333/.373/.641
2016	HOU	MLB	22	217	31	13	3	8	34	15	52	2	0	.264/.313/.478
2017	HOU	MLB	23	626	88	39	5	19	71	55	97	17	5	.284/.352/.475
2018	HOU	MLB	24	705	105	51	1	31	103	96	85	10	4	.286/.394/.532
2019	HOU	MLB	25	675	96	38	3	23	78	73	107	12	4	.272/.359/.463

Breakout: 6%   Improve: 52%   Collapse: 5%   Attrition: 2%   MLB: 100%
Comparables: Anthony Rendon, David Wright, Pablo Sandoval

YEAR	TEAM	LVL	AGE	PA	DRC+	VORP	BABIP	BRR	FRAA	WARP
2016	CCH	AA	22	285	172	38.9	.286	1.6	SS(51): -3.4, 3B(11): 1.4	2.7
2016	FRE	AAA	22	83	161	10.0	.333	-1.2	SS(14): 2.1, LF(3): -0.1	0.8
2016	HOU	MLB	22	217	107	9.6	.317	0.5	3B(40): 0.9, SS(6): -0.1	1.1
2017	HOU	MLB	23	626	114	34.7	.311	-1.5	3B(132): 8.7, SS(30): -2.9	3.9
2018	HOU	MLB	24	705	150	72.6	.289	-1.6	3B(136): 5.4, SS(28): -0.4	7.4
2019	HOU	MLB	25	675	125	37.3	.295	0.0	3B 7, SS 0	4.6

After the projections page, we share a few items about the team's home ballpark. There's the aforementioned diagram of the park's dimensions (including distances to the outfield wall), a few important biographical facts about the stadium, a graphic showing the height of the wall from the left-field pole to the right-field pole, and a table showing three-year park factors for the stadium. The park factors are displayed as indexes where 100 is average, 110 means that the park inflates the statistic in question by 10 percent, and 90 means that the park deflates the statistic in question by 10 percent.

Following the ballpark page, we have a **Personnel** section that lists many of the important decision-makers and upper-level field and operations staff members for the franchise, as well as any former Baseball Prospectus staff members who are currently part of the organization.

Position Players

After all that information and a thoughtful bylined essay covering each team, we present our player comments. Each player is listed with the major-league team who employed him as of early January 2019. If a player changed teams after that point via free agency, trade, or any other method, you'll be able to find them in the book for their previous squad.

First, we cover biographical information (age is as of June 30, 2019) before moving onto the stats themselves. Our statistic columns include standard identifying information like **YEAR**, **TEAM**, **LVL** (level of affiliated play) and **AGE** before getting into the numbers. Next, we provide raw, unstranslated numbers like you might find on the back of your dad's baseball cards: **PA** (plate appearances), **R** (runs), **2B** (doubles), **3B** (triples), **HR** (home runs), **RBI** (runs batted in), **BB** (walks), **K** (strikeouts), **SB** (stolen bases) and **CS** (caught stealing). Then we have unadjusted "slash" statistics: **AVG** (batting average), **OBP** (on-base percentage) and **SLG** (slugging percentage).

Just below the stats box is **PECOTA** data, which is discussed further in a following section. After that, it's on to a pithy and always-informative comment written by a member of the Baseball Prospectus staff, before we cover more stats.

The second text box repeats YEAR, TEAM, LVL, AGE, and PA, then moves on to **DRC+** (Deserved Runs Created Plus), which we described earlier as total offensive expected contribution compared to the league average. Next, one of our oldest active metrics, **VORP** (Value Over Replacement Player), considers offensive production, position and plate appearances. In essence, it is the number of runs contributed beyond what a replacement-level player at the same position would contribute if given the same percentage of team plate appearances. VORP does not consider the quality of a player's defense.

BABIP (batting average on balls in play) tells us how often a ball in play fell for a hit, and can help us identify whether a batter may have been lucky or not ... but note that high BABIPs also tend to follow the great hitters of our time, as well as speedy singles hitters who put the ball on the ground.

The next item is **BRR** (Baserunning Runs), which covers all of a player's baserunning accomplishments which includes (but isn't limited to) swiped bags and failed attempts. Next is **FRAA** (Fielding Runs Above Average), which also includes the number of games previously played at each position noted in parentheses. Multi-position players have only their two most frequent positions listed here, but their total FRAA number reflects all positions played.

Our last column here is **WARP** (Wins Above Replacement Player). WARP estimates the total value of a player, which means for hitters it takes into account hitting runs above average (calculated using the DRC+ model), BRR and FRAA. Then, it makes an adjustment for positions played and gives the player a credit for plate appearances based upon the difference between "replacement level"¬–which is derived from the quality of players added to a team's roster after the start of the season¬–and the league average.

Catchers

Catchers are a special breed, and thus they have earned their own separate box which displays some of the defensive metrics that we've built just for them. As an example, let's check out J.T. Realmuto.

YEAR	TEAM	P. COUNT	FRM RUNS	BLK RUNS	THRW RUNS	TOT RUNS
2016	MIA	18935	-8.5	1.8	2.1	-5.6
2017	MIA	18959	5.3	1.7	1.0	9.1
2018	MIA	16399	-0.4	0.9	0.1	0.4
2019	PHI	18448	-1.4	1.5	0.7	0.8

The **YEAR** and **TEAM** columns match what you'd find in the other stat box. **P. COUNT** indicates the number of pitches thrown while the catcher was behind the plate, including swinging strikes, fouls, and balls in play. **FRM RUNS** is the total run value the catcher provided (or cost) his team by influencing the umpire to call strikes where other catchers did not. **BLK RUNS** expresses the total run value above or below average for the catcher's ability to prevent wild pitches and passed balls. **THRW RUNS** is calculated using a similar model as the previous two statistics, and it measures a catcher's ability to throw out basestealers but also to dissuade them from testing his arm in the first place. It takes into account factors like the pitcher (including his delivery and pickoff move) and baserunner (who could be as fast as Billy Hamilton or as slow as Yonder Alonso). **TOT RUNS** is the sum of all of the previous three statistics.

Pitchers

Let's give our pitchers a turn, using 2018 NL Cy Young winner Jacob deGrom as our example. Take a look at his first stat block: the first line and the **YEAR**, **TEAM**, **LVL** and **AGE** columns are the same as in the position player example earlier.

Here too, we have a series of columns that display raw, unadjusted statistics compiled by the pitcher over the course of a season: **W** (wins), **L** (losses), **SV** (saves), **G** (games pitched), **GS** (games started), **IP** (innings pitched), **H** (hits allowed) and **HR** (home runs allowed). Next we have two statistics that are rates: **BB/9** (walks per nine innings) and **K/9** (strikeouts per nine innings), before returning to the unadjusted **K** (strikeouts).

Next up is **GB%** (ground ball percentage), which is the percentage of all batted balls that were hit in the ground, including both outs and hits. Remember, this is based on observational data and subject to human error, so please approach this with a healthy dose of skepticism.

BABIP (batting average on balls in play) is calculated using the same methodology as it is for position players, but it often tells us more about a pitcher than it does a hitter. With pitchers, a high BABIP is often due to poor defense or bad luck, and can often be an indicator of potential rebound, and a low BABIP may be cause to expect performance regression. (A typical league-average BABIP is close to .290-.300.)

After a witty 150ish words on the player like only Baseball Prospectus's staff can provide, it's on to that second stat block, which repeats the YEAR, TEAM, LVL, and AGE columns. The metrics **WHIP** (walks plus hits per inning pitched) and **ERA**

Pittsburgh Pirates 2019

(earned run average) are old standbys: WHIP measures walks and hits allowed on a per-inning basis, while ERA measures earned runs on a nine-inning basis. Neither of these stats are translated or adjusted.

DRA (Deserved Run Average) was described at length earlier, and measures how many runs the pitcher "deserved" to allow per nine innings. Please note that since we lack all the data points that would make for a "real" DRA for minor-league events, the DRA displayed for minor league partial-seasons is based off of different data. (That data is a modified version of our cFIP metric, which you can find more information about on our website.)

Jacob deGrom   RHP
Born: 06/19/88   Age: 31   Bats: L   Throws: R
Height: 6'4"   Weight: 180   Origin: Round 9, 2010 Draft (#272 overall)

YEAR	TEAM	LVL	AGE	W	L	SV	G	GS	IP	H	HR	BB/9	K/9	K	GB%	BABIP
2016	NYN	MLB	28	7	8	0	24	24	148	142	15	2.2	8.7	143	47%	.312
2017	NYN	MLB	29	15	10	0	31	31	201[1]	180	28	2.6	10.7	239	48%	.305
2018	NYN	MLB	30	10	9	0	32	32	217	152	10	1.9	11.2	269	48%	.281
2019	NYN	MLB	31	13	9	0	31	31	186	145	18	2.3	10.7	221	46%	.286

Breakout: 8%   Improve: 29%   Collapse: 28%   Attrition: 6%   MLB: 85%
Comparables: Erik Bedard, A.J. Burnett, CC Sabathia

YEAR	TEAM	LVL	AGE	WHIP	ERA	DRA	WARP	MPH	FB%	WHF	CSP
2016	NYN	MLB	28	1.20	3.04	3.30	3.5	96.3	59.6	12.1	47.2
2017	NYN	MLB	29	1.19	3.53	3.02	5.7	97.2	55.5	14.5	49.5
2018	NYN	MLB	30	0.91	1.70	2.09	8.0	98.2	52.1	16.3	48.4
2019	NYN	MLB	31	1.02	2.91	3.23	3.9	96.6	54.5	14.8	48.2

Just like with hitters, **WARP** (Wins Above Replacement Player) is a total value metric that puts pitchers of all stripes on the same scale as position players. We use DRA as the primary input for our calculation of WARP. You might notice that relief pitchers (due to their limited innings) may have a lower WARP than you were expecting or than you might see in other WARP-like metrics. WARP does not take leverage into account, just the actions a pitcher performs and the expected value of those actions ... which ends up judging high-leverage relief pitchers differently than you might imagine given their prestige and market value.

MPH gives you the pitcher's 95th percentile velocity for the noted season, in order to give you an idea of what the *peak* fastball velocity a pitcher possesses. Since this comes from our pitch tracking data, it is not publicly available for minor-league pitchers.

Finally, we display the three new pitching metrics we described earlier. **FB%** (fastball percentage) gives you the percentage of fastballs thrown out of all pitches. **WhiffRt** (whiff rate) tells you the percentage of swinging strikes induced out of all pitches. **CS Prob** (called strike probability) expresses the likelihood of all pitches thrown to result in a called strike, after controlling for factors like handedness, umpire, pitch type, count, and location.

PECOTA

All players have PECOTA projections for 2019, as well as a set of other numbers that describe the performance of comparable players according to PECOTA. All projections for 2019 are for the player at the date we went to press in early January and are projected into the league and park context as indicated by the team abbreviation. All PECOTA projected statistics represent a player's projected major-league performance.

The numbers beneath the player's stats–Breakout, Improve, Collapse, Attrition–are part and parcel of the PECOTA projections. They estimate the likelihood of changes in performance relative to the player's previously-established level of production, based on the performance of comparable players:

Breakout Rate is the percent change that a player's production will improve by at least 20 percent relative to the weighted average of his performance over his most recent seasons.

Improve Rate is the percent chance that a player's production will improve at all relative to his baseline performance. A player who is expected to perform just the same as he has in the recent past will have an Improve Rate of 50 percent.

Collapse Rate is the percent chance that a position player's production will decline by at least 25 percent relative to his baseline performance.

Attrition Rate operates on playing time rather than performance. Specifically, it measures the likelihood that a player's playing time will decrease by at least 50 percent relative to his established level.

Breakout Rate and Collapse Rate can sometimes be counterintuitive for players who have already experienced a radical change in performance level. It's also worth noting that the projected decline in a player's rate performances might not be indicative of an expected decline in underlying ability or skill, but could just be an anticipated correction following a breakout season.

MLB% is the percentage of similar players who played in the major leagues in their relevant season.

The final pieces of information are the player's three highest-scoring comparable players as determined by PECOTA. All comparables represent a snapshot of how the listed player was performing at the same age as the current player, so if a 23-year-old pitcher is compared to Bartolo Colon, he's actually being compared to a 23-year-old Colon, not the version that pitched for the Rangers in 2018, nor to Colon's career as a whole.

Pittsburgh Pirates 2019

A few points about pitcher projections. First, we aren't yet projecting peak velocity, so that column will be blank in the PECOTA lines. Second, projecting DRA is trickier than evaluating past performance, because it is unclear how deserving each pitcher will be of his anticipated outcomes. However, we know that another DRA-related statistic–contextual FIP or cFIP–estimates future run scoring very well. So for PECOTA, the projected DRA figures you see are based on the past cFIPs generated by the pitcher and comparable players over time, along with the other factors described above.

Lineouts

In each chapter's Lineouts section, you'll find abbreviated text comments, as well as most of same information you'd find in our full player comments. We limit the stats boxes in this section to only including the 2018 information for each player.

Exclusive Player Visualizations

In our constant battle to provide you with new and interesting baseball content you can't find anywhere else, we've added a trio of data visualizations to each hitter's entry in these books and a pair of visualizations for each pitcher.

For hitters, you'll find three new infographics. The first is each player's **Batted Ball Distribution**, which displays the five major sections of the field: LF (left), LCF (left center), CF (center), RCF (right center), and RF (right). The percentage indicated tells us what percentage of batted balls from that hitter fell within that part of the field during the 2018 season. We've also included the hitter's slugging percentage on balls in play (also called **SLGCON**) for that part of the field.

You'll also see two heatmaps: **Strike Zone vs LHP** and **Strike Zone vs RHP**. These heat maps represent a view of the strike zone from behind the catcher. Areas where there is a darker coloration represent the places where a higher percentage of pitches resulted in hits. In other words, the heatmap represents a hitter's "sweet spots" for getting hits against either left-handed or right-handed pitchers, depending on the image.

Pitchers get two images that help explain what their pitches look like from a hitter's perspective: **Pitch Shape vs LHH** and **Pitch Shape vs RHH**. These images show you the shape and the "tunneling" effect of each pitcher's offerings from the batter's perspective. For each type of pitch that a pitcher throws (represented by an indicator shape), there's a set of dots indicating the flight path, where each dot represents a 0.01-second interval. This maps the average trajectory and speed of an offering, ending where the ball crosses the plate. The solid black box represents the regular strike zone, while the gray contour lines indicate the range of locations that a pitcher typically works in.

Below the image, we provide a bit more detailed information about each pitcher's average offering in the **Pitch Types** box. Here, we also list each of the pitcher's major offerings under the **Type** column.

- **Fastballs** (which usually refers to the four-seam variation)
- **Sinkers** and/or two-seam fastballs
- **Cutters** (which could include "hard" cutters like cut fastballs and "soft" cutters that resemble hard sliders)
- **Changeups** (not including most splitters)
- **Splitters** (split-fingered pitches, forkballs, and some split-changes)
- **Sliders** and/or slurves
- **Curveballs** (including spike-curveballs and knuckle-curveballs, as well as some slurvy curves)
- **Slow curveballs** and/or eephus pitches
- **Knuckleballs**
- **Screwballs**

The **Freq** column indicates the percentage of overall pitches that fall into each of those type categories; if a pitcher has a 16.55% score for changeups, then that's the percent of all pitches that he throws as changeups. **Velo** is exactly what you think it is: the average miles per hour for each pitch type. **H Mov** is the number of inches of horizontal movement on the average pitch of that type, while **V Mov** is the number of inches of vertical movement on the average pitch of that type. (At Baseball Prospectus, we measure this over the long flight of the ball and include gravity into the V Mov number in order to give you the most realistic representation of what the pitch *actually* does.)

If you're wondering about the second number in brackets, that's the index for that velocity or movement compared to the league average. Like DRC+, a score of 100 means that the speed or movement is about the same as league average, while a higher score means that there's higher velocity or movement than the league average. Numbers below 100 indicate less velocity or movement than the league average.

Part 1: Team Analysis

Table for Two: Previewing the 2019 Pittsburgh Pirates

Rob Mains and Matthew Trueblood

ROB MAINS: The 2018 Pirates won 82 games, seven more than the 2017 club. They also drew 1.47 million fans to PNC Park, a decline of 5,380 per game that was the second-worst in the league (thanks Marlins). Obviously, this was a reaction to the McCutchen and Cole deals. But when I look at the offseason–Mercer, Nova, and Harrison gone, Chisenhall and Lyles signed–I don't see a lot that gets people excited. And they play in a division in which the Brewers, Cardinals, and Reds invested in improving their teams in '19. Am I missing something? What makes this a better-than-.500 club?

MATT TRUEBLOOD: Well, I know what the Pirates themselves would say. They'd contend that Joe Musgrove and Chris Archer are both primed for big seasons as they settle into the team's culture and system. They'd point to the strong seasons Trevor Williams and Jameson Taillon had last year, and they'd talk up Mitch Keller as an imminent addition to a high-upside rotation. They'd spin the winter as the calm after the storm, and say that the additions of Archer and Keone Kela in July were their big splashes for 2019. They'd also argue that Gregory Polanco basically reached his ceiling in 2018, before that foolish and clumsy slide wrecked his shoulder and trimmed a bit off both the end of that season and the beginning of this one. They'd say Starling Marte tapped into his power and didn't have to trade contact for it, and that 2019 will be the year he finally becomes a tall drink of Mike Trout.

I even buy some of it. Marte really impressed me in 2018. I just don't trust the pitching infrastructure, or literally any of their infielders. What do you make of this rotation, anyway? I feel like it's the linchpin of whatever it is they're trying to do.

ROB: I agree, and I share your concern. Archer continued to have better peripherals than his ERA would indicate, but not by a lot, and his ERA's risen three straight years. I'm good with Taillon and Williams, especially Taillon, but that's just three starters. Keller was impressive in AA/AAA last year, DRA- of 80, but the hasn't pitched an inning in the majors. The bullpen falls off pretty quickly after

Felipe Vazquez, Kela, and Richard Rodriguez. And ye gods, the offense. Do you see *anybody* on this team as a breakout candidate? I'd like to say Josh Bell but he was out-slugged by Adam Frazier.

MATT: A year ago, I said Frazier, and he sort of lived up to it, so I'll hitch my horse to him for another season. At this point, I'm over the idea that he'll further blossom with more playing time, but I feel a bit less worried that he'll wilt than I might have been a year ago. The other obvious candidate, if you look at it all just right, is Elias Diaz. How do you see them dividing up the catching duties? Anyone I'm missing who can deliver more thump?

ROB: Frazier showed a pretty nice glove at second for a guy who started only 38 games there in the minors. And I'm with you re: Diaz. Cervelli's in the last year of his contract, hasn't played in over 104 games since his first year in Pittsburgh, and is drawing a salary that gives management hives, so Diaz should get some time to play, maybe even a 50/50 split as the season rolls on and Cervelli inevitably gets hurt. I keep holding out hope that Bell breaks out–he's a large human with a higher average exit velocity than Edwin Encarnacion, Anthony Rizzo, Matt Carpenter, and Nolan Arenado, and he's not a crazy GB guy. And I guess we're at the point where a big Polanco season would be seen as *finally* living up to his potential rather than a breakout.

Just as it's hard to figure out a breakout star, I don't see any big candidates for a collapse, do you? I mean, any pitcher could get hurt, and Cervelli's probably a concussion away from retiring (I wonder whether he'd be a good coach), but nobody really scares me. I hope people aren't expecting a replay of Williams' second half (1.38 ERA). PECOTA sees him regressing toward his DRA, which was more than a run higher than his ERA, but being a one-win pitcher doesn't strike me as a collapse.

MATT: Were any of their hitters good enough last year to collapse? Probably not. Corey Dickerson let me down by becoming much more normal last year: he makes more contact in the zone than out of it, still swings at everything, doesn't generate as much improbable power as he used to. He's still weird, but no longer unique, and I think he'll decline slightly.

The big collapse risk, in my opinion, is Felipe Vazquez. He bore very heavy usage in 2016 and 2017, and although Clint Hurdle took his foot off the gas a little in 2018, Vazquez still has 218 appearances and over 220 innings pitched over the last three years.

Eight other guys have racked up at least 210 appearances and 210 innings as relievers from ages 24-26. Armando Benitez, Carlos Marmol, and Bryan Shaw survived that and were fantastic at age 27. Juan Rincon and Braden Looper managed to maintain their (uninspiring) levels of usage and performance for another few years. Jeurys Familia, Kelvin Herrera, and Cla Meredith, however, went downhill rather sharply at 27. I love Vazquez and want to believe he's more Benitez than Herrera, but the evidence cuts both ways.

The era of big data in baseball is obviously just beginning, but the team that sort of brought the revolution about seems to be falling behind. Maybe I'm being too harsh there. Are you encouraged about the changes to the coaching staff? Can they wean themselves off the sinker?

ROB: Mmmmaybe. I look at Ivan Nova for supporting evidence. In 2015 with the Yankees, he threw 45% sinkers. In 2016, 51%. He continued to throw mostly sinkers after the trade to Pittsburgh that year but dropped all the way to 39% in 2017 and 35% last year. Williams' money pitch is his four-seamer. But Archer threw 20 sinkers in 96 innings for Tampa Bay and 206 in 52 1/3 in Pittsburgh last year, so who knows.

Not bringing back the hitting coaches struck me as a bit of a knee-jerk: The team was ninth in runs per game and DRC+ in 2018, which is actually *better* than in 2017 (13th and 12th), and they play in a pitcher's park. But to your point, if the lesson of *Moneyball* is exploiting a market inefficiency, the cat's out of the bag with framing, shifting, and two-seamers. I don't get the sense that the Pirates have found a new inefficiency. (And they're certainly not going to engage the one that's emerged over the last two years, "spending money on your team to make it better.")

MATT: Heh. No, and that's the big, frustrating takeaway. They're a Manny Machado away from having a respectable payroll, and a Manny Machado away from serious playoff consideration. This franchise that has invested so wisely in technology, player development, and the front office arms race just refuses to do the same for actual players.

I agree about the offense not having been all that bad, especially given the injury issues they had. In the end, though, I like the hires they made. We're pretty clearly in the middle of a very rapid change in philosophy that is pervading the sport, and it's not only in Pittsburgh where an effort to stay ahead of the curve has pushed inoffensive personnel out the door. Better that, at least in the current climate, than to wait too long to make a change. (I fear that's exactly what they've done by retaining both Hurdle and Searage.)

Let's look beyond this moment, though. This is a club at a crossroads. As you mentioned, it's not just McCutchen and Cole who are gone now, but Mercer and Harrison and Nova. Without going anywhere near the tanking route, they seem to have embarked on a five-year plan, turning to a longer-term focus over the last year. So, five years from now, what will Pirates fans remember of this team? Is it the beginning of something new, or a continuation of something we didn't realize had begun?

ROB: I really hate to be a pessimist but I don't know whether we're seeing anything resembling a turnaround point. The year a bumper crop of prospects appears on the scene? The Pirates have an decent number of prospects, five, on our Top 101 list, but all but Keller are in the bottom half and guys like Travis Swaggerty and Oneil Cruz are nowhere near the majors. As we've discussed, there aren't a lot of breakout candidates on the team. I don't see them embarking on a 2019 version of *Big Data Baseball*, zigging where everybody else is zagging. And they're certainly not going to spend meaningful money. I could see 2019 as a continuation of the past three years–putting a competent team on the field that, given a ten-win positive variance in some season, could luck into a Wild Card slot. But it won't happen. Am I too negative?

MATT: I think that's the shape of the season that will unfold for them. I see more cause for optimism when I step back a little. You're right that Swaggerty and Cruz won't make splashes this year, and unless Lonnie Chisenhall has his first healthy season in recent memory, the absence of Austin Meadows is going to be felt in a significant way.

On the other hand, I think there's talent here on which too many are giving up too easily. That's Musgrove, maybe. It's Kevins Kramer and Newman. I really like Erik Gonzalez, in a "he could be what Jordy Mercer just was for them, for another five years" kind of way. Vazquez and Kela are a fun back-end tandem, but Richard Rodriguez and Kyle Crick are a fun secondary tandem, too. I think there's a real chance that the story of this season is, especially in hindsight, a happy one—that maybe Bell or Moran goes by the wayside, but that's counterbalanced by really exciting and encouraging seasons from Marte and Polanco and Taillon and Archer. I think this could be a developmental season that does feel like the turning of a corner, leaving a (relatively) fruitful past behind but revealing a more promising future than we've imagined lately. Maybe that's way too pollyanna.

ROB: There's been no division for which the PECOTA projection has generated as much controversy as the NL Central. Currently, the difference between first and last place is eight games, which is 5% over 162 games. So it's all a tossup! We've got the Pirates at 80-82. Where do you see the team ending up, and on what path?

I'll go first. I think PECOTA is being a tad optimistic. I'm thinking something below .500. I could see Archer being, well, what he was last season; Bell and Moran and Polanco being what they were last season; and a pitcher getting hurt, resulting in the team trading somebody–a healthy Cervelli or Dickerson? One of the quartet of bullpen arms you mentioned?–for prospects at the deadline. If I'm wrong, I think it'll be because of the pitching. (Also, not that it's wholly relevant, but I did not realize that Musgrove and Crick are younger than Taillon, Williams, and Vazquez–they really do have some good young arms.)

MATT: I also see a sub-.500 season, but they're going to give some people (especially outside their division) hell in September. You're right that a selloff could come, and artificially depress the win total of a talented team. I keep coming back to the infield. I love infields. I try not to get so sucked into my fascination with them that I base my entire team analysis around them, but the heartbeat of a great team is its infield. This is a 70-win infield. Liking their collection of young arms and longing for the simultaneous Marte/Polanco brilliance that has stubbornly eluded us, I'll call them a 77-win team.

Performance Graphs

2018 Hit List Ranking

Committed Payroll (in millions)

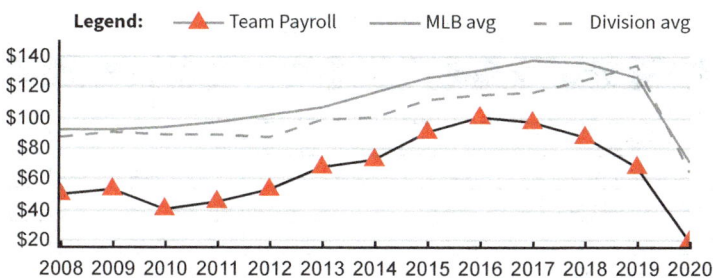

Farm System Ranking

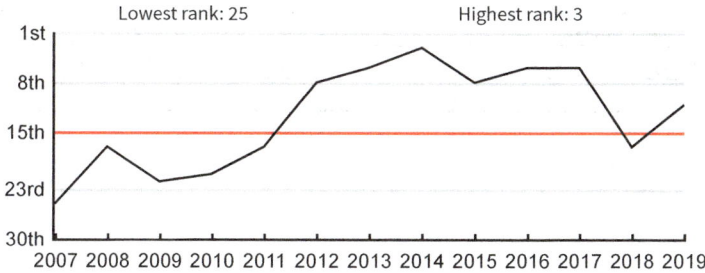

2018 Team Performance

ACTUAL STANDINGS

Team	W	L	Pct
MIL	96	67	.588
CHN	95	68	.582
SLN	88	74	.543
PIT	**82**	**79**	**.509**
CIN	67	95	.413

THIRD-ORDER STANDINGS

Team	W	L	Pct
MIL	93	70	.570
CHN	92	71	.564
SLN	83	79	.512
PIT	**78**	**83**	**.484**
CIN	71	91	.438

TOP HITTERS

Player	WARP
Starling Marte	3.4
Corey Dickerson	2.4
Francisco Cervelli	2.4

TOP PITCHERS

Player	WARP
Jameson Taillon	4.2
Joe Musgrove	2.5
Trevor Williams	2

VITAL STATISTICS

Statistic Name	Value	Rank
Pythagenpat	.499	15th
Runs Scored per Game	4.30	18th
Runs Allowed per Game	4.30	14th
Deserved Runs Created Plus	92	20th
Deserved Run Average	4.17	9th
Fielding Independent Pitching	4.02	14th
Defensive Efficiency Rating	.704	19th
Batter Age	27.9	13th
Pitcher Age	26.5	2nd
Salary	$86.3M	27th
Marginal $ per Marginal Win	$2.2M	27th
Disabled List Days	$696.0M	2nd
$ on DL	9%	4th

2019 Team Projections

PROJECTED STANDINGS

Team	W	L	Pct	+/-
MIL	88	74	.543	-8
SLN	85	77	.524	-3
CIN	81	81	.500	+14
PIT	**80**	**82**	**.493**	**-2**
CHN	79	83	.487	-16

TOP PROJECTED HITTERS

Player	WARP
Starling Marte	3.1
Corey Dickerson	3.0
Adam Frazier	1.7

TOP PROJECTED PITCHERS

Player	WARP
Jameson Taillon	2.7
Chris Archer	2.5
Joe Musgrove	1.5

FARM SYSTEM REPORT

Top Prospect	Number of Top 101 Prospects
Mitch Keller, #18	5

KEY DEDUCTIONS

Player	WARP
Josh Harrison	1.4
Ivan Nova	1.0
Jordan Luplow	1.0
Jordy Mercer	0.7

KEY ADDITIONS

Player	WARP
Lonnie Chisenhall	1.2
Francisco Liriano	0.4
Jordan Lyles	0.4
Melky Cabrera	0.3

Team Personnel

President
Frank Coonelly

EVP, General Manager
Neal Huntington

Assistant General Manager
Kevan Graves

VP, Assistant General Manager
Kyle Stark

Manager
Clint Hurdle

BP Alumni
Dan Fox
Grant Jones

PNC Park Stats

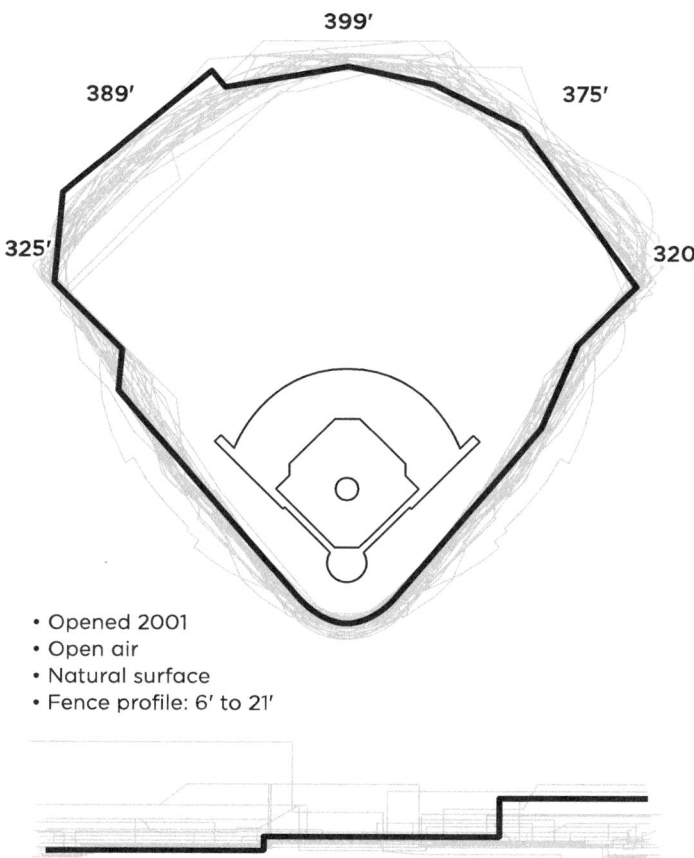

- Opened 2001
- Open air
- Natural surface
- Fence profile: 6' to 21'

Three-Year Park Factors

Runs	Runs/RH	Runs/LH	HR/RH	HR/LH
96	94	100	87	100

Pirates Team Analysis

There were some names I expected to hear, and I did indeed hear them. I asked the population of Pittsburgh Pirates-adjacent people in my life—some coworkers and a comedy writer and some bloggers and an attorney with a podcast, a representation of my social circle at this point in my life such so distressingly apt that I feel compelled to mention it myself—about the bleakest moment in their last 15 or so years as fans of this team. This was not a scientific poll, of course, but writing an essay like this about a team like the Pirates is not a scientific pursuit. It is about a specific type of dread, and there is nothing scientific about dread. The broader vibe of the Pirates is not something that can be quantified, really. It is, as it has been for decades, a fact as obvious and inarguable as weather.

But yes, if you were wondering, Matt Morris came up more than once. In one of the last moves of his disastrous and implausibly long tenure as the team's GM, Dave Littlefield acquired the last $13.5 million of Morris's contract from San Francisco at the trade deadline in 2007, seemingly on a whim; the Bucs sent back a young Rajai Davis and a minor-leaguer-to-be-named who will also remain unnamed here. Littlefield was fired six weeks later, and Morris was released in late April of 2008 after allowing six homers in 22-and-a-third innings. There were also multiple mentions of Daniel Moskos, who was more valuable to the Pirates in a shorter stint with the club than Morris was—which is to say that he was more or less replacement level in the only 31 games he'd ever spend as a big leaguer—but whose legacy is even doomier. Littlefield drafted Moskos, a reliever out of Clemson, fourth overall in 2007's June Draft, because ownership declined to pay the bonus due to Georgia Tech phenom and eventual fifth-overall Matt Wieters; the team subsequently issued a press release noting that Moskos "was ranked by Baseball America as the fifth-best *pitcher* available in the draft."[1]

Derek Bell came up, too, as Derek Bell does; he was the worst of the many veteran free agents that Littlefield reliably snagged on the eve of their expiration dates. Aramis Ramirez, a homegrown star who was dealt away at the beginning of his prime for Bobby Hill—not the pudgy goofus from *King Of The Hill*, but no more valuable during his brief time with the Pirates—was mentioned. So was the Pirates having players from their organization selected with five of the first six picks of the 2003 Rule Five Draft, "resulting in audible laughter in the New Orleans hotel meeting room" as the AP noted in its postmortem on Littlefield's six years with the team[2]; the best of those players was Jose Bautista, whom the team would later re-acquire and then trade again, for a catcher named Robinzon Diaz. No one mentioned Pat Meares, although I long ago got used to people not mentioning Pat Meares as often as I think they should. You are probably getting it by now.

All of this is well-known, not subtext but the actual lurid text itself, for people that care to know things about the Pirates. It also seemed just a few years ago to be something like ancient history. First Cam Bonifay and then Littlefield got some smallish things right and a great many bigger things wrong during their respective unconscionably long stints as GM, but were persistently hamstrung by two different but equally cheap owners; neither did especially well in the job, but both were set up to fail. Neil Huntington, who has been on the job since 2007 and was given a four-year contract extension back in 2017, is different. He got some of the big things right that his predecessors had always gotten wrong and a number of smaller things as well, and subsequently built teams that didn't just win but ranged from endearingly spunky to nearly sublime—few teams have been less well-served by the Wild Card system than the 98-win Pirates of 2015, whose postseason consisted entirely of one brisk manhandling by Jake Arrieta. It was not nearly as long ago as it seems that the Pirates were not just *competitive*, which is the current baseball slang for Decent Enough That No One Is Bringing Guillotines To The Stadium, but actually *good*.

But *good* is expensive, and difficult, and fleeting, and so after the team peaked at 98 wins in 2015 and then declined to pay the necessary cost to get even better Huntington was tasked with taking those teams apart, which he has done in his typical workmanlike fashion since the team's last brief postseason appearance in 2016. Huntington's name came up, too, in the messages I got back from my emissaries to Pirates nation. So, unsurprisingly, did that of Bob Nutting, who has owned the team since 2007. It couldn't have been any other way.

Owners are owners, and problematic for both intrinsic and obvious reasons; Huntington's job, given the constraints placed upon him by ownership, is to do the best he can with whatever chance ownership deigns to give him. He's proven to be pretty good at that fundamentally impossible job, and the Pirates bounced back to a winning record in 2018 and made some trades that promise to keep them both affordable and *competitive* in years to come. None of the players Huntington has recently acquired—affordable demi-ace Chris Archer, reliably cromulent slugger Corey Dickerson, live-armed reliever Keone Kela—came up, and neither did the franchise mainstays he dealt away under ownership-induced duress in exchange for notably less compelling players. The Pirates are back where they've spent these last lost decades, in pursuit of *competitive*, which means that the players are somewhere between incidental and academic. Mostly, of course, they are fungible. They are not there for bigger things, really, but also bigger things are not in play.

On the ghost roster that my correspondents gave back, one name surprised me more than the others, if only because I'd mostly forgotten that he was even with the team. Juan Nicasio was with the Pirates only briefly, but also he has played for six teams in eight big league seasons. He came aboard as a bit of classic Pirates arbitrage, a busted starter with an electric arm and negligible salary who might possibly figure things out under pitching coach Ray Searage. It took a year, but Nicasio did indeed figure it out, just in time for the team's 2017 stretch collapse.

Nicasio was one of the more effective relievers in the National League that year, even as the team slid out of contention. Instead of trading him at the deadline, the Pirates mysteriously let him go to the Phillies on waivers, where he made just two appearances before being dealt to the Cardinals, the team to which Huntington and his ownership had declined to trade him at the deadline. The machinations saved the Pirates about half a million dollars, cost them a pitcher they'd decided they couldn't re-sign—Nicasio, now established as a quality reliever, went on to sign a two-year, $17 million deal with the Mariners—and a shot at the fringe-y prospect that the Phillies got for their role in facilitating the deal. More than that, though, the specific circumstances of his departure clarified a deeper bleakness that fans had long dreaded looking in the face.

When the team declined to improve that nascent juggernaut between 2015 and 2016, it was clear that while the Pirates would do their level best to be *competitive*, they were not quite willing to take the risks required to actually win. This was a slight, but the pettiness of the Nicasio goofery was somehow worse. "It was a small moment, but I think for even a lot of hardcore Pirates fans that was a breaking point," a correspondent wrote. It wasn't just that they weren't trying to win. It was that it wasn't at all clear what they were trying to do, period. The team had given away a player that it had made valuable, and to a divisional rival through an opportunistic proxy team, for "just the most petty, meaningless amount of savings" and nothing else. Those were the comedy writer's words, if you were wondering. So that's about where we are.

⚾   ⚾   ⚾

It's something of a cliché among wised-up sports fans that the worst place for a team to be is in the middle. If you're on top, then you're on top; if you're on the bottom, there's at least some draft-driven opportunity to rebuild and, if the tank is branded properly, to build some perverse-ish Stockholm Syndrome spirit among the fans. The wide space between is not quite the wasteland it's cracked up to be, but it is also vast enough for a team to get lost in and certainly no place to take out a mortgage. After a budget-minded semi-teardown over the winter sent erstwhile cornerstones Andrew McCutchen and Gerrit Cole out of town and brought back a collection of big league-ready but otherwise unremarkable young

Pittsburgh Pirates 2019

players, the Pirates won 82 games in 2018, good for fourth place in the National League Central and not really within hailing distance of the second Wild Card. They were competitive enough, late enough to justify a pair of July moves that brought in actual big league contributors in the bullpen and the rotation. In sum, the team was busy and better than mediocre, and in retrospect significantly less depressing than might have been expected after its offseason sell-off. That's about the size of the team's accomplishments in 2018, but it's not nothing. But also what is it, really?

Or, to reel back the doom and pull in the focus a bit, what is it that the Pittsburgh Pirates are trying to do, let alone trying to *be*, in 2019 and beyond? When the team seemed poised to break through after that brilliant 2015 season—a season in which no regular member of the starting lineup was older than 29 and the team's farm system was rated by BP as eighth-best in the game—the organization instead busily stood pat and so began to decline. They remained *competitive*—they will continue to be competitive, because Huntington is competent in the ways his predecessors were not and because the organization's best homegrown prospects are nearing the bigs—but they made clear that they were not aiming any higher than that.

For much of the Pirates' time in the wilderness it was not really clear what the team was even trying to do. One high draft pick after another flamed out or topped out or disappeared quietly during their umpteenth desolate Gulf Coast League rehab assignment; the players that survived represented the team with dignity as its sole All-Star selection until it came time to pay them what they were worth. The old Littlefieldian illogic—eagerly picking up the millions left on Matt Morris's contract while flipping homegrown stars for Groupons and Bobby Fucking Hill—is blessedly by the boards. It is clear what Huntington is doing, for the most part, and clear that he knows how to do it decently well. The Pirates will develop players, sometimes better and sometimes worse, and then seek to lock them up to team-friendly deals through their arbitration years; they will chase arbitrage opportunities wherever and whenever they find them, with an emphasis on versatility and depth and cost control. More or less every team does this now, of course. The question is whether the Pirates are willing to do more than that, and whether there's any institutional appetite to do more than compete.

In 2019, the Opening Day payroll is expected to once again be among the lowest in the league. Some help is on the way from within the system. Mitch Keller is the only real elite pitching prospect the team has at the moment, but he is indeed an elite pitching prospect. Despite the fact that he hasn't yet hit for much power in games, 2015 first-rounder Ke'Bryan Hayes drew a Josh Donaldson comp from a talent evaluator I spoke to and there are intriguing prospects studded throughout the system. The Major League roster still features a healthy amount of affordable, high-quality talent, and Huntington has done well at adding more of that on the cheap when he can. This is not always about buying low and seeing things other teams don't; the Pirates have stood by the affordable and versatile Korean infielder Jung-Ho Kang despite serial drunk-driving arrests and a sexual assault accusation, seemingly mostly because of how affordable and versatile he is. Cynicism at the top—owner Bob Nutting's family fortune has been estimated at $1.1 billion, which makes him both one of the richer owners in baseball[3] and someone who should be embarrassed to run the payrolls he does—shows up with unpredictable toxicity downstream. That's always the way it works.

The Pirates are not alone in this. Major League Baseball's unofficial Ennui Division has never been more crowded or competitive, with something like a third of MLB teams are not trying any harder or aiming any higher than the Pirates. Some of them are actively trying to get worse, in the hope that this will later make them better. Some are hoping to improve without spending any money on improvements, which is at least ambitious, or to stay roughly the same without upsetting anyone, which is maybe even more so. All of them are trying, very hard, not to get any more expensive. Many of those teams are much less competent in their pursuit of those lustily hedged goals, and led by ownership that's cheaper or more cynical than Nutting. This likely isn't really much comfort to Pirates fans, though. While they're at the top end of the Ennui Division, the Pirates will play their baseball in the National League Central once the weather gets nice enough, and that division is stocked with teams that have shown more organizational will and capacity to go for it.

The Pirates could be both a decent-to-good team and the fourth-best team in their five-team division. They could also be roughly that good and still finish last. It's a good division and baseball is weird like that, but also that doesn't really seem to be the point. Since it is by now quite clear what the Pirates are willing to do as an organization, and more painfully what they are not willing to do, the usual work of setting expectations seems both drearier and easier. All those decades of towering ineptitude have been exorcised, and what's replaced all that strange failure is something more rational and efficient and infinitely better executed, but finally not all that much more satisfying. Everyone involved unquestionably knows what they're doing, but it is also obvious what that is. The Pirates will be competitive, and lord knows they've certainly been much worse. It's the just barely unspoken willingness to leave it all there that stings.

—*David Roth is a senior editor at Deadspin.*

1. Starkey, Joe. "Pirates Must Be Kidding." Trib Live. Accessed 26 December 2018. https://triblive.com/x/pittsburghtrib/sports/columnists/starkey/s_511615.html#axzz2dxVvGEK6

2. AP. "GM Littlefield Out After Another Lost Pirates Season. Accessed 26 December 2018. http://www.espn.com/mlb/news/story?id=3008832

3. Anonymous. "The Ten Richest MLB Owners." CNBC. Accessed 26 December 2018. https://www.cnbc.com/2012/04/03/The-10-Richest-MLB-Owners.html?slide=2

Part 2: Player Analysis

Josh Bell 1B

Born: 08/14/92 Age: 26 Bats: B Throws: R
Height: 6'4" Weight: 235 Origin: Round 2, 2011 Draft (#61 overall)

YEAR	TEAM	LVL	AGE	PA	R	2B	3B	HR	RBI	BB	K	SB	CS	AVG/OBP/SLG
2016	IND	AAA	23	484	57	23	4	14	60	57	74	3	7	.295/.382/.468
2016	PIT	MLB	23	152	18	8	0	3	19	21	19	0	1	.273/.368/.406
2017	PIT	MLB	24	620	75	26	6	26	90	66	117	2	4	.255/.334/.466
2018	PIT	MLB	25	583	74	31	4	12	62	77	104	2	5	.261/.357/.411
2019	PIT	MLB	26	601	68	27	4	18	72	66	112	3	4	.253/.337/.422

Breakout: 7% Improve: 54% Collapse: 6% Attrition: 8% MLB: 98%
Comparables: Logan Morrison, Conor Jackson, James Loney

At first glance, Bell stagnated in 2018. The power he showed in 2017 disappeared. Although he made up for it in other areas, his overall offensive production, while acceptable, was slightly below average for a major-league first baseman. However, after struggling early, Bell was able to make a mechanical adjustment that turned his season around in the second half. Then-Pirates hitting coach Jeff Branson identified a timing issue and coaxed Bell to get his front foot down earlier, allowing him to make contact sooner and drive the ball like he was doing in 2017. There isn't enough data to know if the change will stick, but the talent is there. If Bell can combine his superb batting eye with a sustainable power stroke, Pittsburgh could finally see Bell's immense potential translate to on-the-field results for a full season.

YEAR	TEAM	LVL	AGE	PA	DRC+	VORP	BABIP	BRR	FRAA	WARP
2016	IND	AAA	23	484	147	24.1	.328	-4.0	1B(96): -3.4, RF(4): 1.3	1.8
2016	PIT	MLB	23	152	102	6.4	.294	0.2	1B(23): -0.3, RF(16): -2.3	0.0
2017	PIT	MLB	24	620	108	19.2	.278	-3.7	1B(147): -6.5	0.5
2018	PIT	MLB	25	583	101	19.2	.305	-0.8	1B(137): -6.8	0.1
2019	PIT	MLB	26	601	104	14.3	.287	-1.5	1B -6	0.9

Josh Bell, continued

Batted Ball Distribution

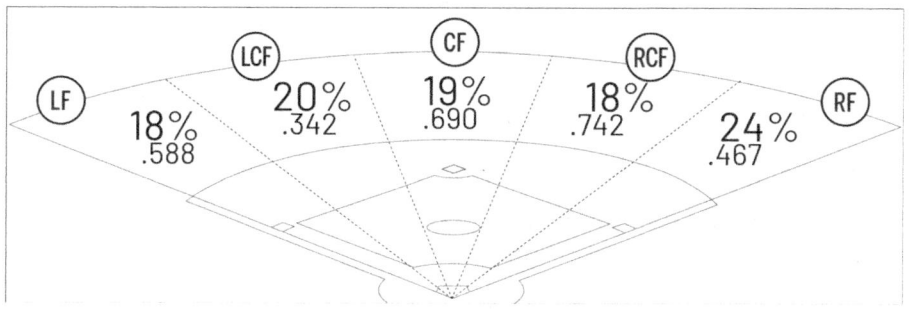

Strike Zone vs LHP

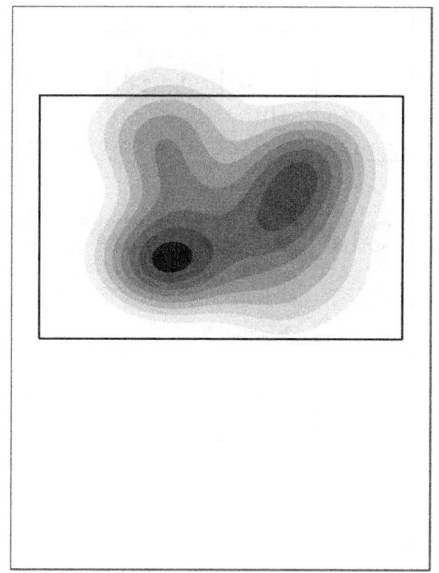

Strike Zone vs RHP

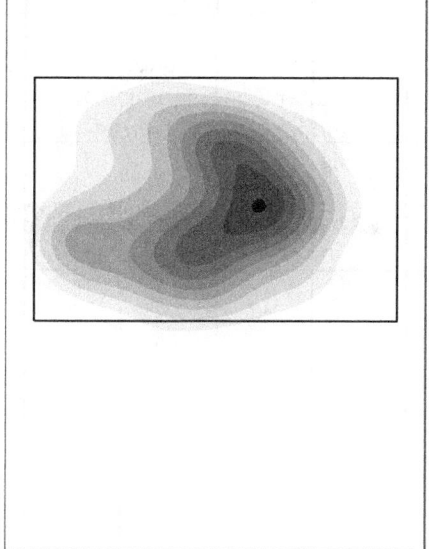

Pittsburgh Pirates 2019

Melky Cabrera OF
Born: 08/11/84   Age: 34   Bats: B   Throws: L
Height: 5'10"   Weight: 210   Origin: International Free Agent, 2001

YEAR	TEAM	LVL	AGE	PA	R	2B	3B	HR	RBI	BB	K	SB	CS	AVG/OBP/SLG
2016	CHA	MLB	31	646	70	42	5	14	86	47	69	2	0	.296/.345/.455
2017	CHA	MLB	32	428	54	17	0	13	56	25	52	0	0	.295/.336/.436
2017	KCA	MLB	32	238	24	13	2	4	29	11	22	1	2	.269/.303/.399
2018	COH	AAA	33	80	7	6	1	0	8	2	10	2	0	.321/.338/.423
2018	CLE	MLB	33	278	28	17	0	6	39	20	38	1	1	.280/.335/.420
2019	PIT	MLB	34	352	35	19	2	7	40	24	50	1	1	.273/.327/.409

Breakout: 0%   Improve: 34%   Collapse: 23%   Attrition: 17%   MLB: 87%
Comparables: Shane Victorino, Tommy Holmes, Rip Radcliff

Cabrera looked like a potential casualty of the chilly 2017-2018 free agent market, another member of the fraternity of players who transitioned directly from "player the White Sox were counting on to get them into the playoffs" to "out of baseball." But with Cleveland's outfield woes, the veteran was pressed into service and he produced a classic Good Contact And Not Much Else Adequate season. ("GCANMEA" if you want to make a new statistic, it's what we do here. Melky will undoubtedly sign out this acronym with arm gestures from first base after a ringing single at some point.) He somehow turned only 34 in August and he plays with endearing joy, so he may keep producing this way for a little while longer.

YEAR	TEAM	LVL	AGE	PA	DRC+	VORP	BABIP	BRR	FRAA	WARP
2016	CHA	MLB	31	646	110	15.7	.314	-4.3	LF(147): -6.6	1.3
2017	CHA	MLB	32	428	97	8.6	.310	-2.2	LF(92): -5.7	0.1
2017	KCA	MLB	32	238	98	-0.3	.280	0.6	RF(46): -6.3, LF(12): -0.6	-0.2
2018	COH	AAA	33	80	110	1.2	.368	-1.0	RF(10): 0.4, LF(6): 0.9	0.2
2018	CLE	MLB	33	278	100	6.2	.303	-0.4	RF(68): 1.7, LF(4): 0.0	0.7
2019	PIT	MLB	34	352	100	8.5	.302	-1.1	RF -5, LF 0	0.3

Melky Cabrera, continued

Batted Ball Distribution

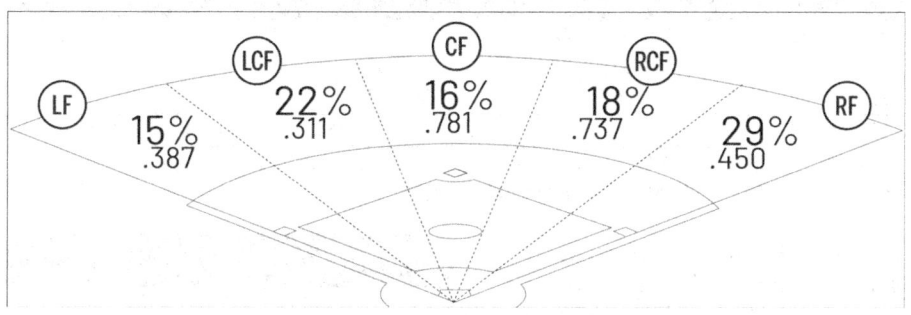

Strike Zone vs LHP   **Strike Zone vs RHP**

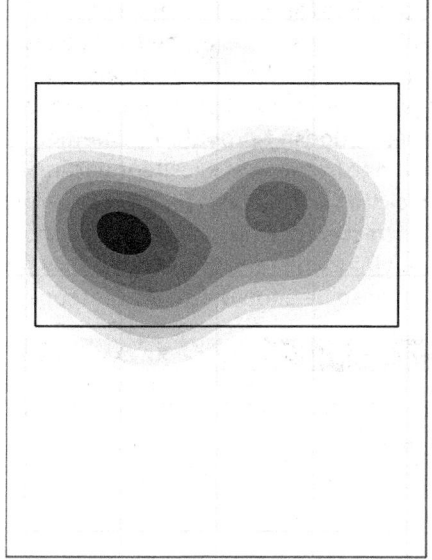

Francisco Cervelli C

Born: 03/06/86 Age: 33 Bats: R Throws: R
Height: 6'1" Weight: 210 Origin: International Free Agent, 2003

YEAR	TEAM	LVL	AGE	PA	R	2B	3B	HR	RBI	BB	K	SB	CS	AVG/OBP/SLG
2016	PIT	MLB	30	393	42	14	1	1	33	56	72	6	2	.264/.377/.322
2017	PIT	MLB	31	304	31	13	2	5	31	32	65	0	2	.249/.342/.370
2018	PIT	MLB	32	404	39	15	3	12	57	51	84	2	3	.259/.378/.431
2019	PIT	MLB	33	469	51	19	2	9	48	53	101	3	2	.246/.348/.371

Breakout: 4% Improve: 36% Collapse: 13% Attrition: 7% MLB: 92%
Comparables: Sherm Lollar, Miguel Montero, Bob Brenly

Even by catching standards, Cervelli is a late bloomer, so it should come as no surprise that he was late to the most recent hip trend. A ground-ball hitter throughout his Pittsburgh tenure—Cervelli had more than two grounders for each fly ball from 2015 to 2017—he started lifting the ball last year. The early returns were impressive, but after eight home runs in his first 42 games, Cervelli regressed, hitting only four in his final 234 plate appearances. No matter how much power Cervelli does or doesn't provide, or whether he's truly lost the ability to be an above-average framer, his excellent batting eye continued to elevate him above the backstop bourgeoisie in 2018. Entering the last year of a three-year, $31 million contract extension, Cervelli has been a bargain by any yardstick. Because of his long injury history, Cervelli can't be relied upon for 130-plus games, but even at 100 or so he should see another top-10 WARP season at the position.

YEAR	TEAM	P. COUNT	FRM RUNS	BLK RUNS	THRW RUNS	TOT RUNS
2016	PIT	13232	13.0	-1.9	-2.4	7.4
2017	PIT	10368	-6.0	0.5	-1.0	-6.8
2018	PIT	13072	-5.8	-1.1	0.6	-6.5
2019	PIT	15404	-4.9	-1.2	-0.9	-7.0

YEAR	TEAM	LVL	AGE	PA	DRC+	VORP	BABIP	BRR	FRAA	WARP
2016	PIT	MLB	30	393	92	16.6	.329	-2.9	C(95): 10.5, 1B(2): -0.1	2.3
2017	PIT	MLB	31	304	91	12.1	.311	-2.9	C(78): -5.6	0.3
2018	PIT	MLB	32	404	116	33.3	.308	0.7	C(94): -3.9, 1B(5): -0.1	2.4
2019	PIT	MLB	33	469	101	20.6	.305	-0.9	C -7, 1B 0	1.2

Francisco Cervelli, continued

Batted Ball Distribution

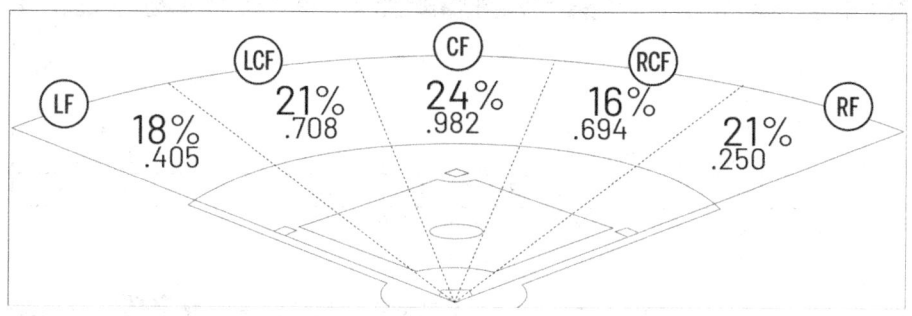

Strike Zone vs LHP   Strike Zone vs RHP

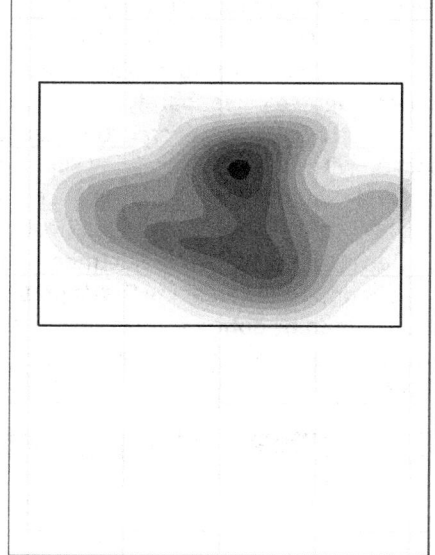

Elias Diaz   C

Born: 11/17/90   Age: 28   Bats: R   Throws: R
Height: 6'1"   Weight: 215   Origin: International Free Agent, 2008

YEAR	TEAM	LVL	AGE	PA	R	2B	3B	HR	RBI	BB	K	SB	CS	AVG/OBP/SLG
2016	PIT	MLB	25	4	0	0	0	0	1	0	1	0	0	.000/.000/.000
2016	IND	AAA	25	97	4	3	0	0	10	3	17	1	0	.266/.289/.298
2017	IND	AAA	26	229	19	10	0	2	27	9	36	3	0	.266/.298/.339
2017	PIT	MLB	26	200	18	14	0	1	19	11	38	1	0	.223/.265/.314
2018	PIT	MLB	27	277	33	12	0	10	34	21	40	0	1	.286/.339/.452
2019	PIT	MLB	28	199	19	8	1	4	21	12	38	1	0	.245/.293/.364

Breakout: 6%   Improve: 45%   Collapse: 9%   Attrition: 36%   MLB: 84%
Comparables: Brayan Pena, Jason Jaramillo, Rob Johnson

Gushing write-ups and purple prose about player breakouts are typically reserved for high-profile prospects who took longer than expected to develop and eventually turned into superstars. Diaz's metamorphosis from a marginal backup into a quality major-league receiver barely registered any notice, even in the Steel City, but he went from being a punchless backup with mediocre receiving skills to a catcher with pop and, um, mediocre receiving skills. Despite amassing a mere 277 plate appearances and rating as an average defender, Diaz was the 15th-best catcher in baseball by WARP thanks to his newfound power. An adjustment led to a cleaner approach at the plate, with a slight uppercut replacing Diaz's previously level swing. These one-year changes can be ephemeral, but while framing is the contemporary buzzword for catcher value, having someone who can swing the lumber at a weak position helps as well.

YEAR	TEAM	P. COUNT	FRM RUNS	BLK RUNS	THRW RUNS	TOT RUNS
2016	PIT	141	0.0	0.0	0.0	0.5
2017	IND	7000	1.3	-0.4	0.8	1.2
2017	PIT	6832	-5.1	-0.7	0.2	-6.2
2018	PIT	9111	-1.2	-2.0	0.1	-3.2
2019	PIT	6208	-2.5	-0.8	0.1	-3.2

YEAR	TEAM	LVL	AGE	PA	DRC+	VORP	BABIP	BRR	FRAA	WARP
2016	PIT	MLB	25	4	97	-0.9	.000	0.0	C(1): 0.1	0.0
2016	IND	AAA	25	97	78	-1.1	.325	-1.0	C(25): -2.2	-0.2
2017	IND	AAA	26	229	89	2.2	.311	-1.2	C(50): 6.3	0.9
2017	PIT	MLB	26	200	62	-4.8	.273	-0.9	C(55): -3.8	-0.4
2018	PIT	MLB	27	277	113	21.0	.302	0.5	C(70): 0.6	1.9
2019	PIT	MLB	28	199	84	5.2	.283	-0.3	C -2	0.2

Elias Diaz, continued

Batted Ball Distribution

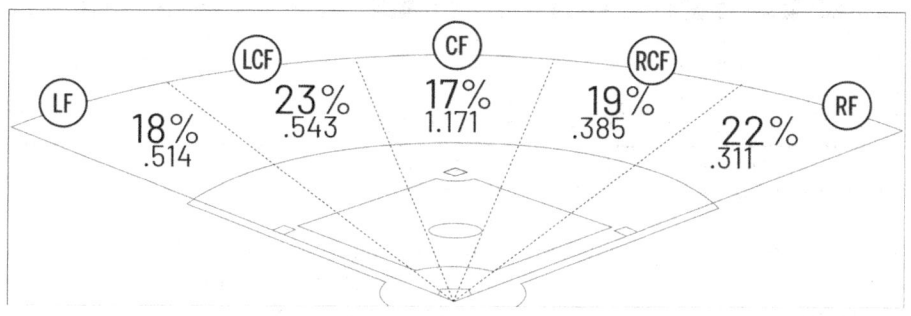

Strike Zone vs LHP

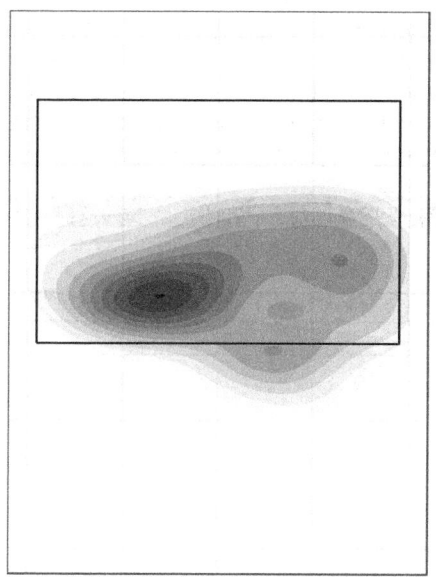

Strike Zone vs RHP

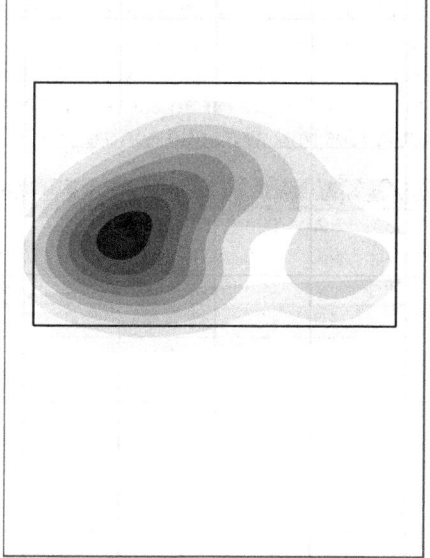

Corey Dickerson LF

Born: 05/22/89 Age: 30 Bats: L Throws: R
Height: 6'1" Weight: 200 Origin: Round 8, 2010 Draft (#260 overall)

YEAR	TEAM	LVL	AGE	PA	R	2B	3B	HR	RBI	BB	K	SB	CS	AVG/OBP/SLG
2016	TBA	MLB	27	548	57	36	3	24	70	33	134	0	2	.245/.293/.469
2017	TBA	MLB	28	629	84	33	4	27	62	35	152	4	3	.282/.325/.490
2018	PIT	MLB	29	533	65	35	7	13	55	21	80	8	3	.300/.330/.474
2019	PIT	MLB	30	545	62	32	4	17	69	34	112	5	3	.270/.320/.451

Breakout: 2%   Improve: 41%   Collapse: 19%   Attrition: 10%   MLB: 100%
Comparables: Yoenis Cespedes, Irish Meusel, Craig Monroe

If you blinked, you might have missed it when Dickerson was designated for assignment by the Rays last winter, taking them off the hook for paying him $5.95 million. Conventional wisdom suggested some team would claim Dickerson at that price, and the Pirates bit, flipping Daniel Hudson's contract and $1 million for Dickerson's services. Known as a free-swinging, bad-ball hitter, Dickerson radically changed his approach in Pittsburgh, laying off high fastballs and cutting his strikeout rate by nine percentage points as a result. He made significant changes on the other side of the ball as well, winning a Gold Glove backed up by both the scouting reports and the defensive metrics. This would have made for an excellent star turn had Dickerson maintained his power, but leaves him as a solid contributor who seldom gets the respect he deserves.

YEAR	TEAM	LVL	AGE	PA	DRC+	VORP	BABIP	BRR	FRAA	WARP
2016	TBA	MLB	27	548	101	7.5	.285	-1.5	LF(76): 4.2, RF(2): -0.3	1.4
2017	TBA	MLB	28	629	109	25.0	.338	-1.9	LF(93): 13.4	3.2
2018	PIT	MLB	29	533	106	16.7	.333	-4.1	LF(124): 10.7	2.4
2019	PIT	MLB	30	545	103	17.0	.316	-0.5	LF 11	3.0

Corey Dickerson, continued

Batted Ball Distribution

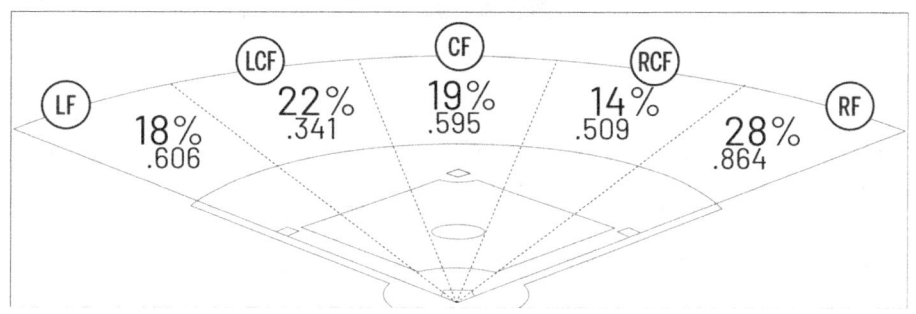

Strike Zone vs LHP

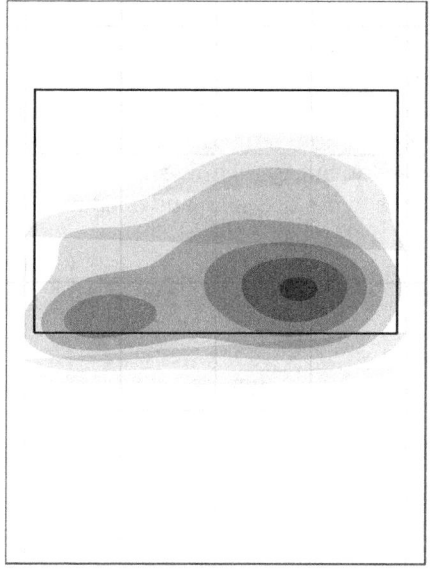

Strike Zone vs RHP

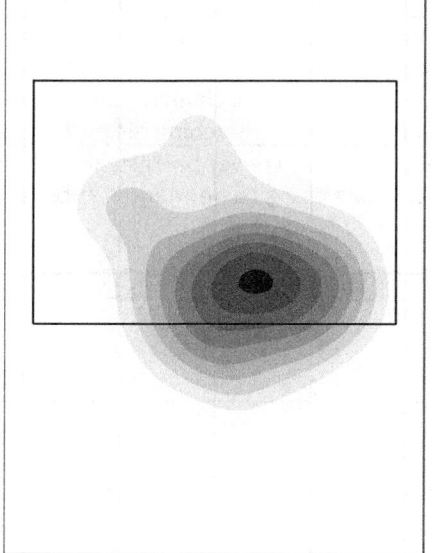

Adam Frazier 2B

Born: 12/14/91   Age: 27   Bats: L   Throws: R
Height: 5'10"   Weight: 180   Origin: Round 6, 2013 Draft (#179 overall)

YEAR	TEAM	LVL	AGE	PA	R	2B	3B	HR	RBI	BB	K	SB	CS	AVG/OBP/SLG
2016	IND	AAA	24	299	34	16	4	0	22	29	27	17	15	.333/.401/.425
2016	PIT	MLB	24	160	21	8	1	2	11	12	26	4	1	.301/.356/.411
2017	PIT	MLB	25	454	55	20	6	6	53	36	57	9	5	.276/.344/.399
2018	IND	AAA	26	137	10	5	2	0	18	11	20	1	3	.223/.289/.298
2018	PIT	MLB	26	352	52	23	2	10	35	29	53	1	3	.277/.342/.456
2019	PIT	MLB	27	556	70	28	4	12	54	43	87	9	7	.271/.335/.415

Breakout: 6%   Improve: 44%   Collapse: 10%   Attrition: 15%   MLB: 98%
Comparables: Alberto Callaspo, Kolten Wong, Logan Forsythe

It's difficult to shed a label or move past a commonly held belief long after it has outlived its usefulness. Mention Frazier and the word "scrappy" comes to mind, primarily because he was never seen as much of a prospect despite decent minor-league results and because his size makes him look like a utility infielder out of central casting in 1975. Frazier was that guy during a minor-league career where he stole a few bases every year but failed to pop more than two dingers at any minor-league level. After hinting at it in 121 games during 2017, he flipped that script in 2018, claiming the Pirates' second base job after Josh Harrison got hurt and nearly matching his professional career home run total in barely 350 PA. Frazier will never be mistaken for a superstar, but every now and then someone cast as a permanent substitute rises to the occasion and becomes more.

YEAR	TEAM	LVL	AGE	PA	DRC+	VORP	BABIP	BRR	FRAA	WARP
2016	IND	AAA	24	299	148	26.5	.369	-1.3	LF(44): 2.0, CF(17): -3.1	1.7
2016	PIT	MLB	24	160	97	6.4	.353	-2.3	LF(20): -0.7, 2B(17): -0.7	0.0
2017	PIT	MLB	25	454	96	18.0	.306	1.3	LF(52): 2.8, 2B(42): -2.6	1.1
2018	IND	AAA	26	137	73	-2.3	.262	-0.9	2B(17): 0.0, RF(7): -0.6	-0.4
2018	PIT	MLB	26	352	104	21.3	.305	1.7	2B(55): 2.5, LF(14): 0.7	1.6
2019	PIT	MLB	27	556	101	19.8	.302	-1.1	2B 0, CF -1	1.7

Adam Frazier, continued

Batted Ball Distribution

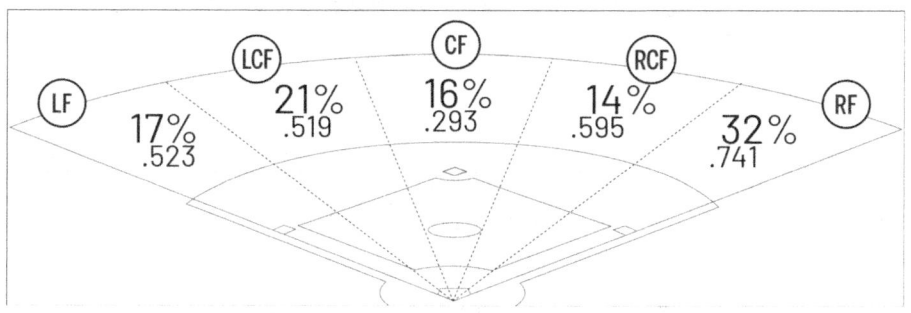

Strike Zone vs LHP

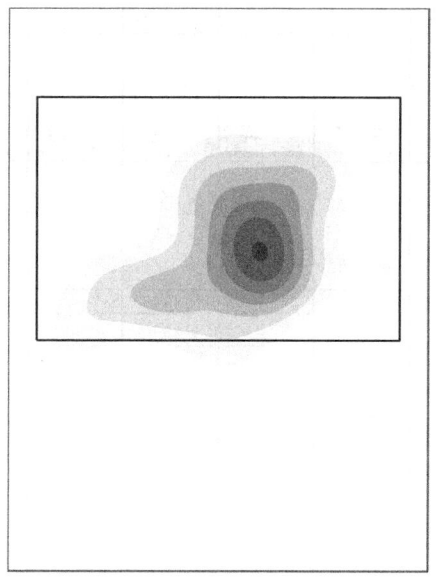

Strike Zone vs RHP

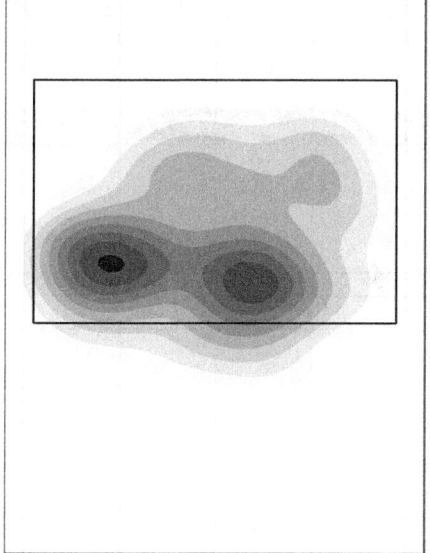

Pittsburgh Pirates 2019

Erik Gonzalez INF
Born: 08/31/91   Age: 27   Bats: R   Throws: R
Height: 6'3"   Weight: 195   Origin: International Free Agent, 2008

YEAR	TEAM	LVL	AGE	PA	R	2B	3B	HR	RBI	BB	K	SB	CS	AVG/OBP/SLG
2016	COH	AAA	24	460	62	31	1	11	53	19	88	12	10	.296/.329/.450
2016	CLE	MLB	24	17	2	0	0	0	0	1	8	0	1	.313/.353/.313
2017	COH	AAA	25	170	21	4	3	6	13	7	53	5	1	.256/.286/.431
2017	CLE	MLB	25	115	18	6	0	4	11	3	37	1	2	.255/.272/.418
2018	CLE	MLB	26	143	17	10	1	1	16	5	34	3	0	.265/.301/.375
2019	PIT	MLB	27	418	44	19	2	10	41	19	108	8	4	.236/.275/.372

Breakout: 9%   Improve: 37%   Collapse: 11%   Attrition: 32%   MLB: 77%
Comparables: Tim Beckham, Tyler Greene, Jason Donald

Gonzalez is the epitome of a stopgap utility player, as he bounced between Cleveland and Columbus for a majority of the last three seasons. He can play all four infield positions as well as the corner outfield spots in a pinch while not killing you with the bat, which is more valuable than ever with shortened benches. But utility will only get you so far, particularly when he's as allergic to taking walks as he's been, and that role is probably as far as he can be stretched him unless he's a last resort for a really rough shortstop situation.

YEAR	TEAM	LVL	AGE	PA	DRC+	VORP	BABIP	BRR	FRAA	WARP
2016	COH	AAA	24	460	114	27.3	.349	0.5	SS(90): 0.2, 2B(8): -1.5	1.9
2016	CLE	MLB	24	17	60	0.2	.625	0.1	SS(8): 0.0, 2B(5): -0.1	0.0
2017	COH	AAA	25	170	74	2.7	.343	0.3	SS(26): -0.7, 2B(9): -0.5	-0.2
2017	CLE	MLB	25	115	65	-1.3	.343	-1.0	2B(36): -0.5, SS(11): 0.1	-0.3
2018	CLE	MLB	26	143	73	3.8	.347	1.9	2B(30): 2.0, 3B(20): 0.9	0.5
2019	PIT	MLB	27	418	72	1.5	.295	-0.1	SS 0, 2B 0	0.0

Erik Gonzalez, continued

Batted Ball Distribution

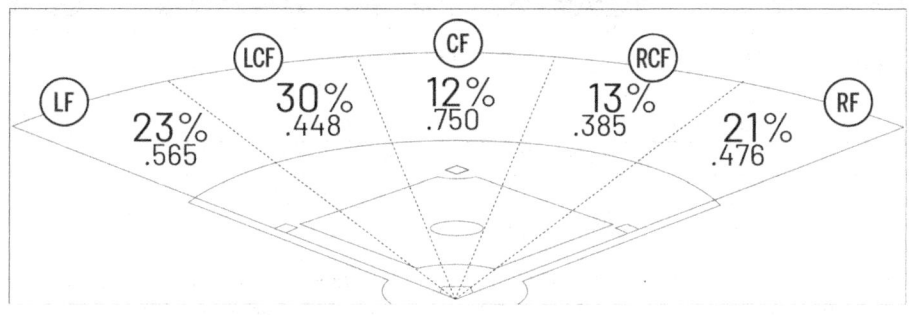

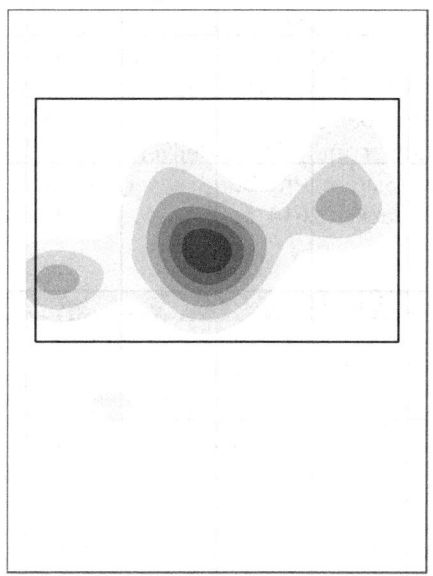

Strike Zone vs LHP

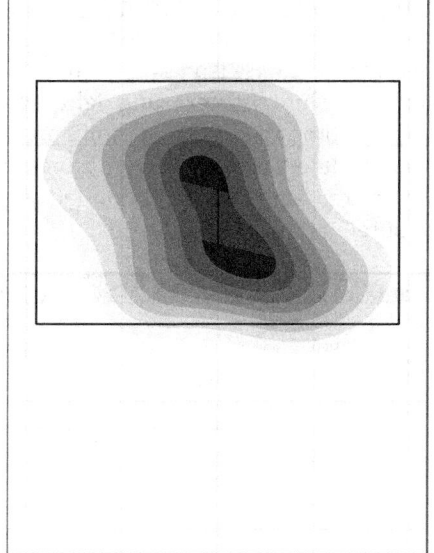

Strike Zone vs RHP

Pittsburgh Pirates 2019

Starling Marte CF
Born: 10/09/88   Age: 30   Bats: R   Throws: R
Height: 6'1"   Weight: 190   Origin: International Free Agent, 2007

YEAR	TEAM	LVL	AGE	PA	R	2B	3B	HR	RBI	BB	K	SB	CS	AVG/OBP/SLG
2016	PIT	MLB	27	529	71	34	5	9	46	23	104	47	12	.311/.362/.456
2017	IND	AAA	28	40	4	1	0	1	3	2	8	3	0	.333/.400/.444
2017	PIT	MLB	28	339	48	7	2	7	31	20	63	21	4	.275/.333/.379
2018	PIT	MLB	29	606	81	32	5	20	72	35	109	33	14	.277/.327/.460
2019	PIT	MLB	30	609	79	28	4	15	64	40	120	36	12	.268/.327/.414

Breakout: 1%   Improve: 36%   Collapse: 17%   Attrition: 7%   MLB: 100%
Comparables: Shane Mack, Adam Jones, Aaron Rowand

The overwrought narrative surrounding performance-enhancing drugs arguably took another hit last year, as Marte delivered the same level of performance in his first full season post-suspension as he has throughout his major-league career. Marte even reached a career high in home runs, something you're not supposed to be able to do after you've been pinched for juicing. Even factoring in the 80 games he missed in 2017 for ingesting something called Nandrolone, Marte has been one of the ten best outfielders in baseball since his first full season in 2013. He isn't off the charts in any particular area, but his all-around game puts him the next rung right below baseball's best. Marte moved to center field full-time this year and didn't miss a beat, continuing to deliver above-average defense but now from a premium position. Pittsburgh wisely locked him into a club-friendly, option-laden deal back in 2014, making it certain he'll be surefire bargain into his 30s.

YEAR	TEAM	LVL	AGE	PA	DRC+	VORP	BABIP	BRR	FRAA	WARP
2016	PIT	MLB	27	529	103	32.2	.380	4.9	LF(114): 7.5, CF(16): -0.4	2.8
2017	IND	AAA	28	40	115	4.7	.407	0.9	LF(6): -0.4, CF(1): 0.1	0.2
2017	PIT	MLB	28	339	91	10.9	.324	3.4	LF(56): 5.9, CF(25): 3.1	1.8
2018	PIT	MLB	29	606	107	36.7	.312	0.1	CF(139): 7.0	3.4
2019	PIT	MLB	30	609	102	28.1	.315	3.6	CF 2	3.1

Starling Marte, continued

Batted Ball Distribution

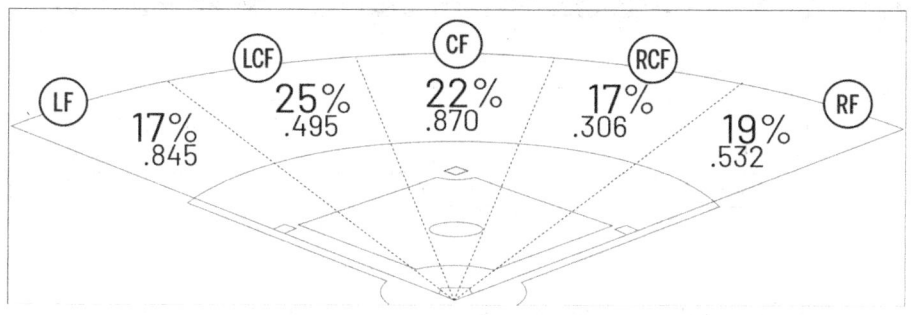

Strike Zone vs LHP   **Strike Zone vs RHP**

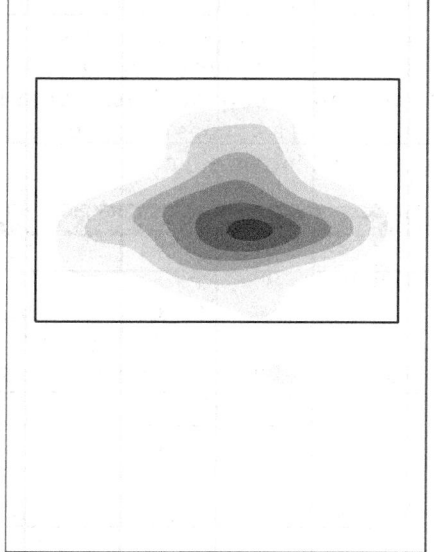

Colin Moran 3B

Born: 10/01/92 Age: 26 Bats: L Throws: R
Height: 6'4" Weight: 205 Origin: Round 1, 2013 Draft (#6 overall)

YEAR	TEAM	LVL	AGE	PA	R	2B	3B	HR	RBI	BB	K	SB	CS	AVG/OBP/SLG
2016	FRE	AAA	23	511	50	18	1	10	69	47	124	3	2	.259/.329/.368
2016	HOU	MLB	23	25	1	1	0	0	2	1	8	0	0	.130/.200/.174
2017	FRE	AAA	24	338	53	15	1	18	63	31	55	0	3	.308/.373/.543
2017	HOU	MLB	24	12	3	0	1	1	3	1	1	0	0	.364/.417/.818
2018	PIT	MLB	25	465	49	19	1	11	58	39	82	0	2	.277/.340/.407
2019	PIT	MLB	26	356	40	14	1	11	41	29	75	1	1	.246/.312/.399

Breakout: 12% Improve: 46% Collapse: 4% Attrition: 17% MLB: 73%
Comparables: Andy Marte, Conor Gillaspie, Michael Morse

Moran was freed from what we described as "purgatory" in last winter's *Annual* when the Pirates acquired him as part of an underwhelming package for Gerrit Cole. Moran wasn't supplanting Alex Bregman at the hot corner in Houston unless Bregman fell down a large well—and perhaps not even then—so the trade gave him what he has always needed: an opportunity to play. Ultimately, Moran was a second-division regular at third base whose defensive prowess is only going to get worse from here, just as the scouts foretold. Moran should continue to get opportunities, but he's likely to be the kind of player whose role is questioned if he finds himself on a contending team. For better or worse, that likely buys him some time.

YEAR	TEAM	LVL	AGE	PA	DRC+	VORP	BABIP	BRR	FRAA	WARP
2016	FRE	AAA	23	511	84	5.0	.332	-4.6	3B(109): 5.1, SS(2): -0.3	0.0
2016	HOU	MLB	23	25	70	-3.4	.200	0.1	3B(8): 0.8	0.1
2017	FRE	AAA	24	338	136	27.8	.323	-0.3	3B(57): 0.3, 1B(15): -1.7	1.8
2017	HOU	MLB	24	12	97	2.5	.333	0.6	1B(4): -0.1, 3B(3): -0.2	0.0
2018	PIT	MLB	25	465	100	22.3	.316	-1.5	3B(116): -2.7	1.2
2019	PIT	MLB	26	356	92	5.5	.290	-0.8	3B -1	0.4

Colin Moran, continued

Batted Ball Distribution

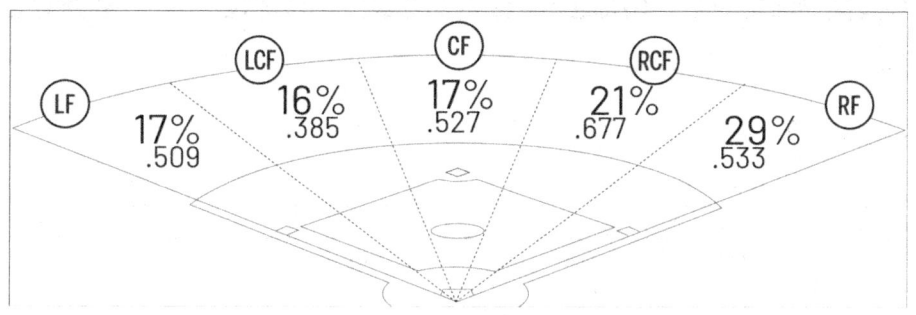

Strike Zone vs LHP **Strike Zone vs RHP**

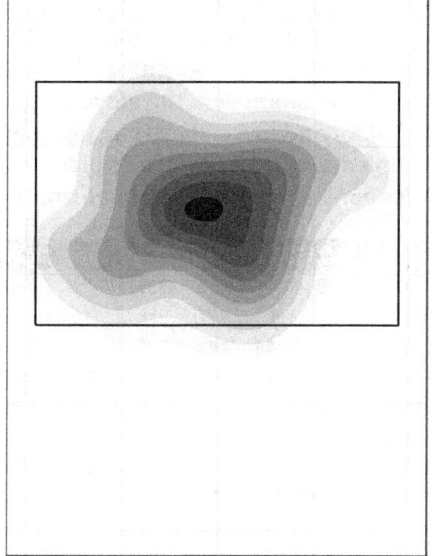

Pittsburgh Pirates 2019

Kevin Newman SS

Born: 08/04/93 Age: 25 Bats: R Throws: R
Height: 6'1" Weight: 180 Origin: Round 1, 2015 Draft (#19 overall)

YEAR	TEAM	LVL	AGE	PA	R	2B	3B	HR	RBI	BB	K	SB	CS	AVG/OBP/SLG
2016	BRD	A+	22	189	24	10	1	3	24	17	12	4	1	.366/.428/.494
2016	ALT	AA	22	268	41	11	2	2	28	26	24	6	3	.288/.361/.378
2017	ALT	AA	23	375	42	18	2	4	30	22	40	4	2	.259/.310/.359
2017	IND	AAA	23	178	23	11	2	0	11	7	22	7	1	.283/.314/.373
2018	IND	AAA	24	477	74	30	2	4	35	31	50	28	11	.302/.350/.407
2018	PIT	MLB	24	97	7	2	0	0	6	4	23	0	1	.209/.247/.231
2019	PIT	MLB	25	378	39	17	1	6	33	21	58	9	4	.238/.285/.344

Breakout: 15%   Improve: 60%   Collapse: 1%   Attrition: 42%   MLB: 72%
Comparables: Brock Holt, Dixon Machado, Brian Dozier

Hello, Newman. After three and a half years in the minors, he finally made it to the Pirates for a September cup of coffee and a Drake's Coffee Cake (not the Junior. This was your big boy). The profile hasn't changed since Newman was drafted in the first round back in 2015. He has an excellent feel for hitting but his swing generates virtually no power. The defense is acceptable at shortstop, but if you're going to run an empty .275 batting average out there every day you want Ozzie Smith with the glove as opposed to "acceptable." Newman has the high floor and low ceiling that, like many young Pirates, fits the mold of a complementary player. If he's lucky, his career will last long enough to get a "nice game, pretty boy" from an angry fan on the gravely road behind PNC Park.

YEAR	TEAM	LVL	AGE	PA	DRC+	VORP	BABIP	BRR	FRAA	WARP
2016	BRD	A+	22	189	193	28.1	.375	1.4	SS(38): 1.4	2.4
2016	ALT	AA	22	268	111	14.8	.308	2.3	SS(60): 0.3	1.3
2017	ALT	AA	23	375	92	14.2	.282	1.4	SS(81): 0.6	0.7
2017	IND	AAA	23	178	85	4.9	.324	-1.3	SS(38): 0.4	0.2
2018	IND	AAA	24	477	122	32.8	.333	3.2	SS(83): 2.9, 2B(21): -0.6	3.0
2018	PIT	MLB	24	97	62	-4.2	.275	-0.6	SS(24): -1.4, 2B(8): -0.7	-0.3
2019	PIT	MLB	25	378	72	2.5	.267	0.2	SS 0, 2B 0	0.0

Kevin Newman, continued

Batted Ball Distribution

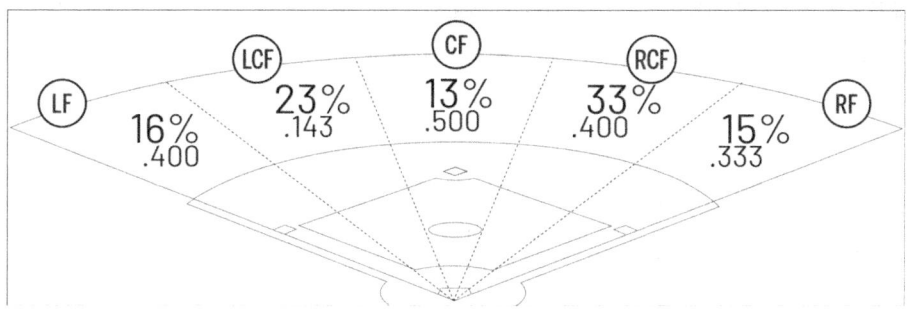

Strike Zone vs LHP   *Strike Zone vs RHP*

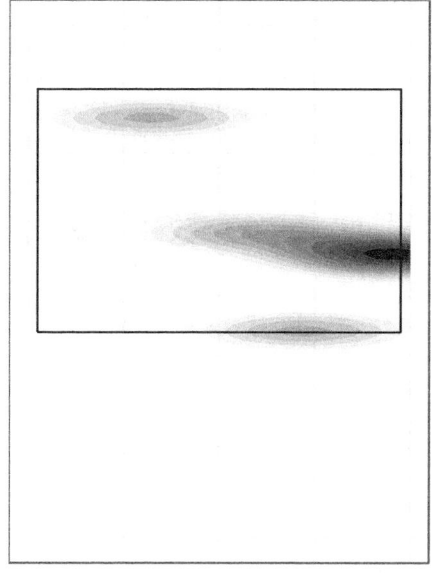 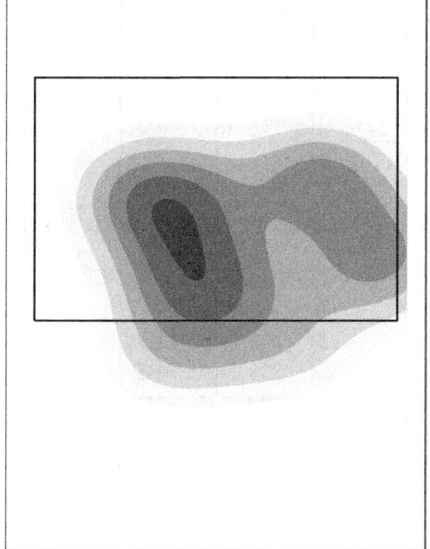

Pittsburgh Pirates 2019

Jose Osuna 4C

Born: 12/12/92   Age: 26   Bats: R   Throws: R
Height: 6'3"   Weight: 240   Origin: International Free Agent, 2009

YEAR	TEAM	LVL	AGE	PA	R	2B	3B	HR	RBI	BB	K	SB	CS	AVG/OBP/SLG
2016	ALT	AA	23	283	34	18	3	6	38	23	44	1	1	.269/.329/.435
2016	IND	AAA	23	234	27	19	1	7	31	13	36	2	3	.291/.333/.482
2017	IND	AAA	24	41	6	5	0	0	1	5	9	1	1	.250/.341/.389
2017	PIT	MLB	24	227	31	13	4	7	30	9	40	0	0	.233/.269/.428
2018	IND	AAA	25	342	45	26	0	9	59	31	51	5	3	.321/.378/.497
2018	PIT	MLB	25	111	14	9	0	3	11	3	22	0	0	.226/.252/.396
2019	PIT	MLB	26	157	17	9	1	4	17	10	30	1	0	.248/.299/.407

Breakout: 12%   Improve: 44%   Collapse: 7%   Attrition: 24%   MLB: 71%
Comparables: Danny Valencia, Michael Morse, Andy Marte

Throughout his career, the knock on Osuna has been he's limited to first base on the defensive side of the spectrum and his bat can't carry him there. The Pirates decided to throw caution to the wind and tried Osuna out at third base, first in the minors and then in September as part of a platoon with Colin Moran. The experiment partially worked. Moran and Osuna both hit well, but their defense at the hot corner resembled Roger Dorn's in the first half of *Major League*. While versatility will never hurt any player's chances at landing a bench job, Osuna needs to show far more with the bat for the Pirates to overlook his deficiencies with the leather.

YEAR	TEAM	LVL	AGE	PA	DRC+	VORP	BABIP	BRR	FRAA	WARP
2016	ALT	AA	23	283	94	8.3	.298	0.3	1B(55): -3.2, RF(9): -0.4	-0.6
2016	IND	AAA	23	234	129	8.8	.322	0.3	1B(27): 0.9, LF(24): 3.9	1.3
2017	IND	AAA	24	41	115	1.2	.333	0.1	1B(6): -0.2, RF(2): 0.0	0.1
2017	PIT	MLB	24	227	78	-1.3	.254	-0.7	RF(25): -0.4, 1B(23): -1.1	-0.3
2018	IND	AAA	25	342	156	30.5	.353	1.4	3B(47): 4.6, 1B(24): -0.7	3.4
2018	PIT	MLB	25	111	80	0.6	.256	0.8	1B(12): 1.9, 3B(7): -0.2	0.3
2019	PIT	MLB	26	157	94	3.0	.280	-0.3	1B -1, RF 0	0.2

Jose Osuna, continued

Batted Ball Distribution

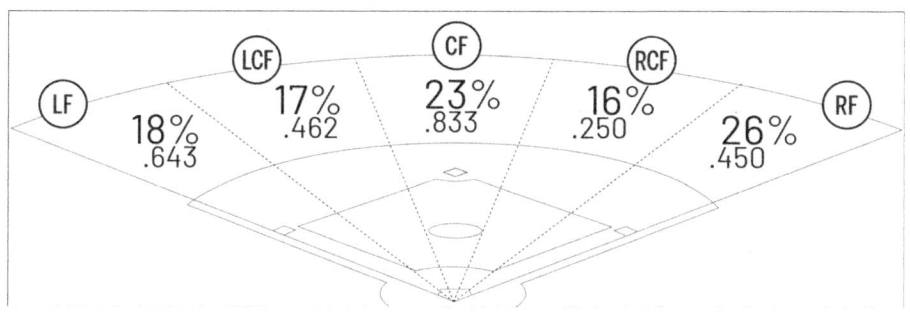

Strike Zone vs LHP   **Strike Zone vs RHP**

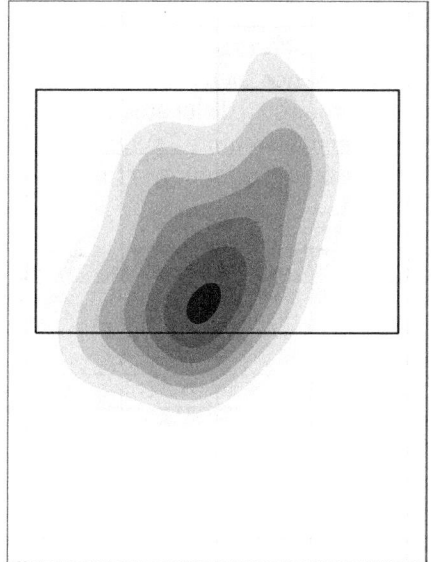 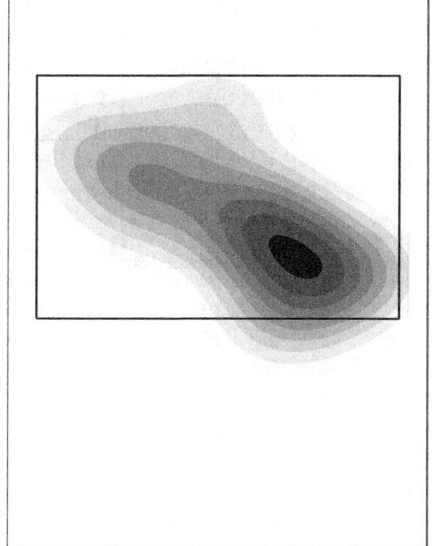

Pirates Player Analysis - 43

Gregory Polanco RF

Born: 09/14/91 Age: 27 Bats: L Throws: L
Height: 6'5" Weight: 235 Origin: International Free Agent, 2009

YEAR	TEAM	LVL	AGE	PA	R	2B	3B	HR	RBI	BB	K	SB	CS	AVG/OBP/SLG
2016	PIT	MLB	24	587	79	34	4	22	86	53	119	17	6	.258/.323/.463
2017	PIT	MLB	25	411	39	20	0	11	35	27	60	8	1	.251/.305/.391
2018	PIT	MLB	26	535	75	32	6	23	81	61	117	12	2	.254/.340/.499
2019	PIT	MLB	27	426	53	22	3	14	52	38	85	11	3	.255/.325/.438

Breakout: 1% Improve: 50% Collapse: 20% Attrition: 12% MLB: 97%
Comparables: Alex Rios, Gerardo Parra, Jason Heyward

Some high-end prospects show up in the majors and take the world by storm. Others take years to convert their considerable promise into results. Polanco fell in the latter camp, mixing flashes of brilliance with stretches of disappointing performance that made some wonder if he would ever live up to the hype that made him a top-25 prospect heading into his rookie season. In 2018, he didn't exactly struggle out of the gate, but a .201 batting average and league-average production through May 30 didn't inspire confidence, either. Then Polanco took off, with a .287/.359/.557 slash from May 31 until his season ended on September 7 with a bone bruise in his left knee. Polanco then became the personification of the game Operation. Doctors repaired a dislocated shoulder and, in the process, discovered a damaged labrum that required surgery. We won't find out if Polanco's strong finish in 2018 was the beginning of his star turn until the 2019 season is well under way.

YEAR	TEAM	LVL	AGE	PA	DRC+	VORP	BABIP	BRR	FRAA	WARP
2016	PIT	MLB	24	587	98	19.6	.291	-1.0	RF(111): 9.8, LF(29): 0.1	2.0
2017	PIT	MLB	25	411	87	3.4	.272	0.5	RF(68): 4.1, LF(25): -2.6	0.5
2018	PIT	MLB	26	535	107	29.2	.287	0.7	RF(124): 1.3	1.8
2019	PIT	MLB	27	426	105	15.2	.291	1.1	RF 1	1.6

Gregory Polanco, continued

Batted Ball Distribution

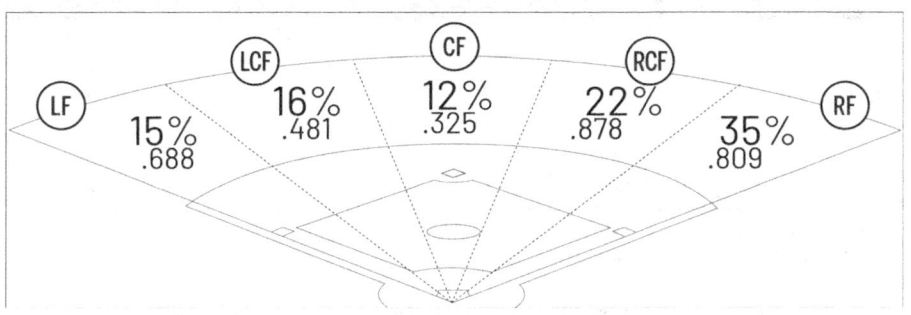

Strike Zone vs LHP	Strike Zone vs RHP
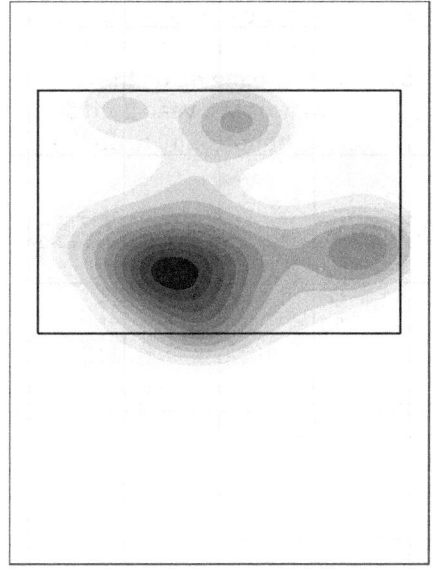	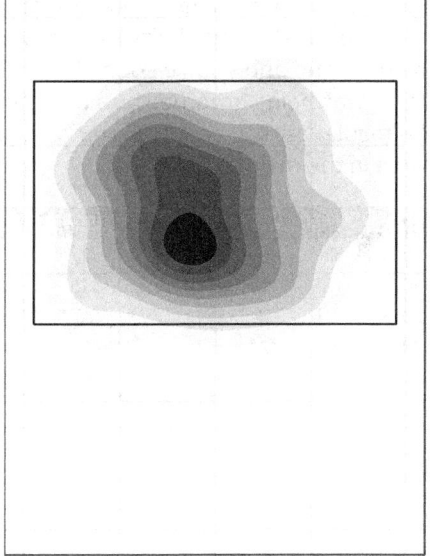

Pablo Reyes OF

Born: 09/05/93 Age: 25 Bats: R Throws: R
Height: 5'8" Weight: 170 Origin: International Free Agent, 2012

YEAR	TEAM	LVL	AGE	PA	R	2B	3B	HR	RBI	BB	K	SB	CS	AVG/OBP/SLG
2016	BRD	A+	22	355	41	20	1	5	45	37	47	13	8	.265/.341/.386
2017	ALT	AA	23	483	62	21	3	10	50	51	70	21	14	.274/.356/.410
2018	ALT	AA	24	49	3	3	0	0	5	4	5	3	0	.244/.306/.311
2018	IND	AAA	24	398	52	20	4	8	36	28	71	13	7	.289/.341/.435
2018	PIT	MLB	24	63	9	2	0	3	7	5	11	0	1	.293/.349/.483
2019	PIT	MLB	25	103	13	4	1	3	10	7	21	2	1	.245/.301/.404

Breakout: 7%   Improve: 31%   Collapse: 2%   Attrition: 26%   MLB: 49%
Comparables: Phil Ervin, Chris Pettit, Trevor Crowe

Reyes is an organizational soldier who marched on Pittsburgh, defying long odds as an unheralded and undrafted free agent out of the Dominican Republic in 2012 to make his major league debut last September. Reyes is the kind of player both scouts and projection systems see as "future replacement level," but all he has done since his professional debut as a 17-year-old is rake. Add some decent base-stealing ability and the versatility to play almost any position on the diamond and you've got a player who is deservedly banging on the door. Reyes was being groomed as a utility player in the minors last year, both during the regular season and in winter ball, and will get the opportunity to do the same in the majors.

YEAR	TEAM	LVL	AGE	PA	DRC+	VORP	BABIP	BRR	FRAA	WARP
2016	BRD	A+	22	355	117	15.8	.293	1.5	SS(36): 3.8, 2B(35): -2.2	1.3
2017	ALT	AA	23	483	115	27.6	.306	-0.4	2B(71): 3.9, CF(31): 1.6	1.8
2018	ALT	AA	24	49	86	-0.3	.275	-0.2	CF(7): -0.7, 2B(3): 0.0	-0.1
2018	IND	AAA	24	398	116	18.5	.338	1.2	LF(42): 3.6, 3B(27): 2.1	1.4
2018	PIT	MLB	24	63	101	4.2	.318	0.4	RF(8): 2.0, LF(6): 0.7	0.5
2019	PIT	MLB	25	103	87	1.5	.269	0.0	3B 0, LF 1	0.2

Pablo Reyes, continued

Batted Ball Distribution

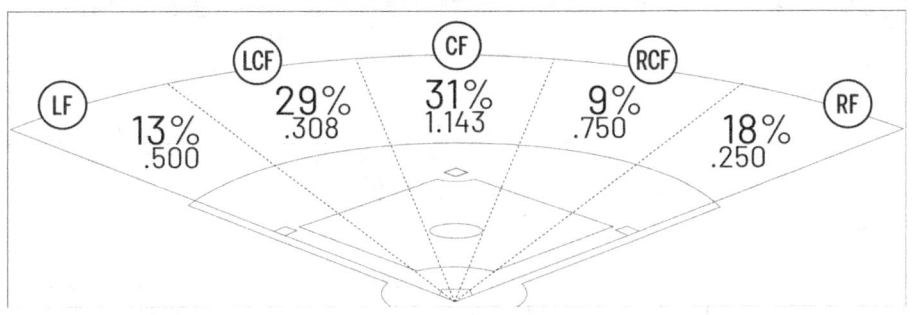

Strike Zone vs LHP   **Strike Zone vs RHP**

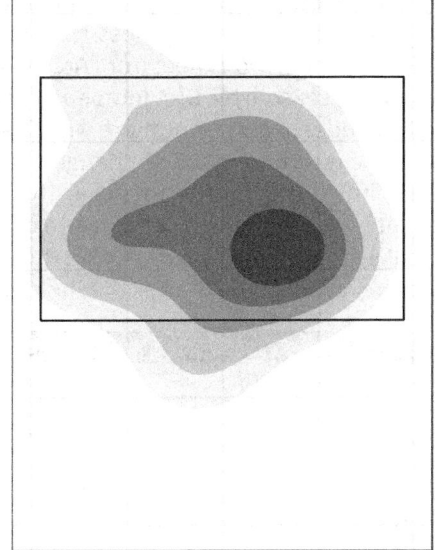

Chris Archer   RHP

Born: 09/26/88   Age: 30   Bats: R   Throws: R
Height: 6'2"   Weight: 195   Origin: Round 5, 2006 Draft (#161 overall)

YEAR	TEAM	LVL	AGE	W	L	SV	G	GS	IP	H	HR	BB/9	K/9	K	GB%	BABIP
2016	TBA	MLB	27	9	19	0	33	33	201[1]	183	30	3.0	10.4	233	49%	.297
2017	TBA	MLB	28	10	12	0	34	34	201	193	27	2.7	11.1	249	43%	.325
2018	TBA	MLB	29	3	5	0	17	17	96	102	11	2.9	9.6	102	46%	.343
2018	PIT	MLB	29	3	3	0	10	10	52[1]	53	8	3.1	10.3	60	48%	.328
2019	PIT	MLB	30	10	9	0	28	28	159	144	16	2.8	9.5	169	45%	.299

Breakout: 15%   Improve: 49%   Collapse: 24%   Attrition: 5%   MLB: 97%
Comparables: Tim Lincecum, Kenta Maeda, Matt Garza

It's impossible to discuss Archer without the obligatory mention of how much better his DRA is than his ERA, and to desperately search for reasons why. As was the case when Charlie Day ranted about the existence of Pepe Silvia, reason frequently gives way to irrationality and dubious connections are established that make no sense whatsoever to the informed observer. While Archer has frequently outperformed his peripherals, he finally went from being somewhat unlucky to simply having a less-than-stellar season in 2018. The high strikeout rate we've come to expect from Archer wasn't there, and for the first time since his rookie season, his DRA jumped over four. An abdominal strain sidelined the right-hander in June, but there wasn't a discernable performance improvement when he returned in July. A change of scenery via a trade to Pittsburgh didn't help either. It's tempting to go full Charlie and cover a wall with reams of paper, bright red lines and arrows to figure out if 2018 was the new normal for Archer, but it's more likely it was a blip on the radar and Archer continues to perform like the reliable no. 2 starter that he always has been.

YEAR	TEAM	LVL	AGE	WHIP	ERA	DRA	WARP	MPH	FB%	WHF	CSP
2016	TBA	MLB	27	1.24	4.02	3.38	4.6	97.1	48.5	13.4	45.4
2017	TBA	MLB	28	1.26	4.07	3.53	4.6	97.4	47.4	14.6	47.4
2018	TBA	MLB	29	1.39	4.31	4.12	1.3	96.5	45.6	14.3	48.6
2018	PIT	MLB	29	1.36	4.30	4.30	0.6	96.6	49.3	13.2	45.6
2019	PIT	MLB	30	1.22	3.44	3.75	2.4	96.2	47.4	14	46.8

Chris Archer, continued

Pitch Shape vs LHH

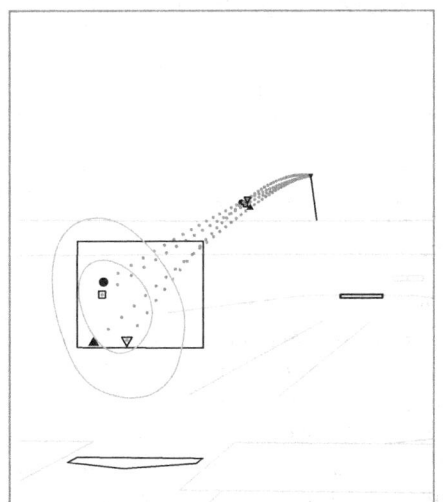

Pitch Shape vs RHH

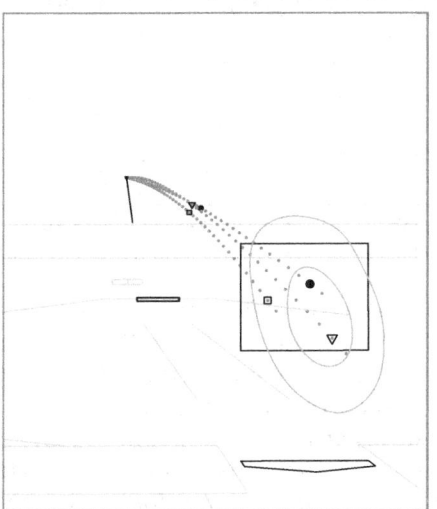

Type		Frequency	Velocity	H Movement	V Movement
●	Fastball	37.9%	95.3 [109]	-5 [108]	-11.5 [114]
☐	Sinker	9.0%	95.3 [114]	-10.2 [120]	-13.8 [122]
+	Cutter				
▲	Changeup	9.9%	88.2 [111]	-10.6 [103]	-23.6 [111]
✕	Splitter				
▽	Slider	41.6%	88.5 [118]	4.7 [99]	-31.3 [105]
◇	Curveball	1.5%	82.3 [114]	4.9 [87]	-43.2 [111]
⊕	Slow Curveball				
✳	Knuckleball				
▼	Screwball				

Steven Brault LHP

Born: 04/29/92   Age: 27   Bats: L   Throws: L
Height: 6'0"   Weight: 200   Origin: Round 11, 2013 Draft (#339 overall)

YEAR	TEAM	LVL	AGE	W	L	SV	G	GS	IP	H	HR	BB/9	K/9	K	GB%	BABIP
2016	IND	AAA	24	2	7	0	16	15	71^1	66	6	4.4	10.2	81	39%	.319
2016	PIT	MLB	24	0	3	0	8	7	33^1	45	5	4.6	7.8	29	47%	.354
2017	IND	AAA	25	10	5	0	21	20	120^1	85	5	3.3	8.2	109	53%	.252
2017	PIT	MLB	25	1	0	1	11	4	34^2	41	3	3.6	6.0	23	45%	.317
2018	PIT	MLB	26	6	3	0	45	5	91^2	84	10	5.6	8.1	82	50%	.289
2019	PIT	MLB	27	3	3	0	51	0	54	47	4	4.7	8.8	53	46%	.288

Breakout: 23%   Improve: 39%   Collapse: 20%   Attrition: 21%   MLB: 77%
Comparables: Alex Colome, Adam Warren, Bryan Mitchell

The highlight of Brault's season came on June 19 against the Milwaukee Brewers. Brault didn't take the mound that day but the microphone, belting out a beautiful rendition of the national anthem in full uniform. Unfortunately for the Pirates, very little about Brault's 2018 was pitch perfect. He picked up some velocity on his fastball but not enough to keep hitters guessing. On August 3, Brault's season struck a minor key, as the Pirates demoted him to Triple-A. It's been the same sad song for Brault throughout his big-league career, and unless something changes his appearances for Pittsburgh will be nothing but music to opposing batters' ears.

YEAR	TEAM	LVL	AGE	WHIP	ERA	DRA	WARP	MPH	FB%	WHF	CSP
2016	IND	AAA	24	1.42	3.91	3.46	1.5				
2016	PIT	MLB	24	1.86	4.86	5.13	0.1	93.8	67.3	11.1	44.6
2017	IND	AAA	25	1.07	1.94	4.01	2.2				
2017	PIT	MLB	25	1.59	4.67	6.17	-0.3	93.6	72	8.8	46.8
2018	PIT	MLB	26	1.54	4.61	5.66	-0.7	94.7	65	10.8	46.9
2019	PIT	MLB	27	1.37	4.00	4.31	0.3	93.9	67.6	10.6	46.8

Steven Brault, continued

Pitch Shape vs LHH

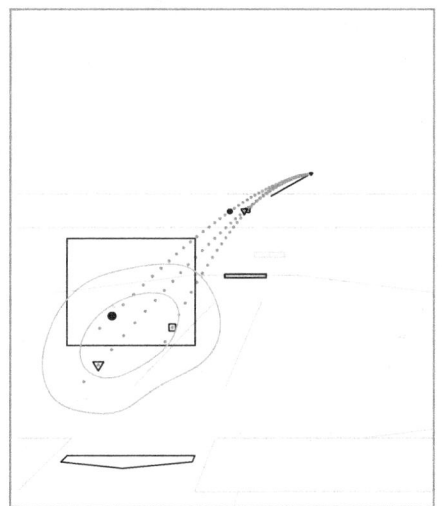

Pitch Shape vs RHH

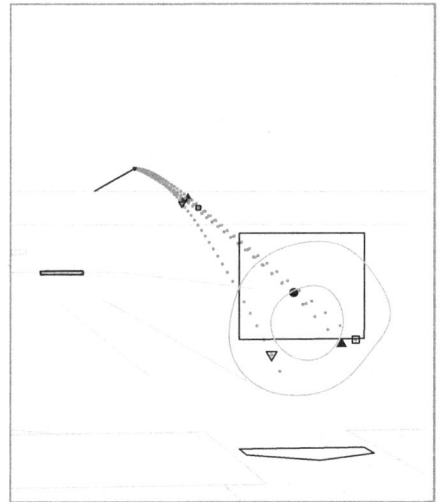

Type		Frequency	Velocity	H Movement	V Movement
●	Fastball	43.8%	93.4 [103]	9.2 [88]	-16 [99]
☐	Sinker	21.2%	92.8 [102]	13.9 [90]	-22.3 [94]
+	Cutter				
▲	Changeup	13.0%	86 [103]	12 [96]	-29.7 [93]
✕	Splitter				
▽	Slider	19.2%	86.9 [111]	-3.4 [94]	-29.2 [111]
◇	Curveball	2.9%	79.2 [103]	-9.4 [107]	-41.8 [114]
⊕	Slow Curveball				
✱	Knuckleball				
▼	Screwball				

Kyle Crick RHP

Born: 11/30/92   Age: 26   Bats: L   Throws: R
Height: 6'4"   Weight: 220   Origin: Round 1, 2011 Draft (#49 overall)

YEAR	TEAM	LVL	AGE	W	L	SV	G	GS	IP	H	HR	BB/9	K/9	K	GB%	BABIP
2016	RIC	AA	23	4	11	0	23	23	109	110	8	5.5	7.1	86	46%	.311
2017	SAC	AAA	24	1	2	6	24	0	29^1	24	1	4.0	12.0	39	45%	.329
2017	SFN	MLB	24	0	0	0	30	0	32^1	22	2	4.7	7.8	28	39%	.233
2018	PIT	MLB	25	3	2	2	64	0	60^1	45	3	3.4	9.7	65	43%	.268
2019	PIT	MLB	26	2	2	0	46	0	48	43	5	4.7	9.7	53	42%	.295

Breakout: 21%   Improve: 46%   Collapse: 16%   Attrition: 16%   MLB: 70%
Comparables: Esmerling Vasquez, Jeremy Jeffress, Keyvius Sampson

As sometimes happens with pitchers drafted out of high school, Crick devolved from a high-upside arm scouts and fantasy players dream on to a long-term project only a pitching coach could love. The Pirates inherited that project from the Giants last winter, grabbing Crick as part of the package for Andrew McCutchen. The results in his first full major-league season were okay. Literally. Despite a glittering ERA, cFIP pegged Crick as a league-average reliever. Though, for him, 2018 wasn't about a miraculous turnaround but rather about establishing himself as a viable major-league option both now and in the future. Crick did exactly that, harnessing more control than he's ever shown while still touching in the mid-90s on the gun and turning into a bit of a righty killer. Maybe Ray Searage will coax more than this out of Crick, but the 2018 version of Crick remains more than anyone was expecting at the end of his Giants tenure.

YEAR	TEAM	LVL	AGE	WHIP	ERA	DRA	WARP	MPH	FB%	WHF	CSP
2016	RIC	AA	23	1.62	5.04	3.79	1.7				
2017	SAC	AAA	24	1.26	2.76	2.74	0.8				
2017	SFN	MLB	24	1.21	3.06	4.29	0.3	96.7	74.5	12.1	45.7
2018	PIT	MLB	25	1.13	2.39	4.41	0.4	97.4	72.9	12.6	47.9
2019	PIT	MLB	26	1.40	4.13	4.43	0.2	96.8	74.7	12.7	47.8

Kyle Crick, continued

Pitch Shape vs LHH

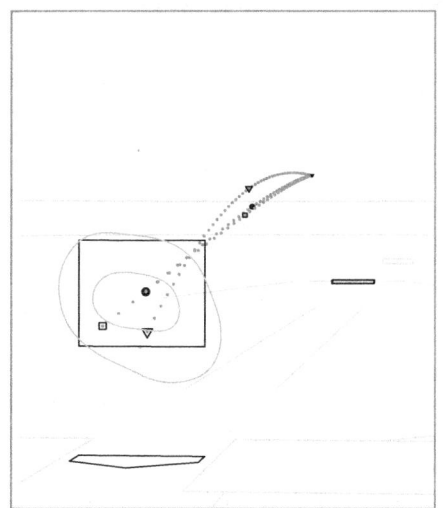

Pitch Shape vs RHH

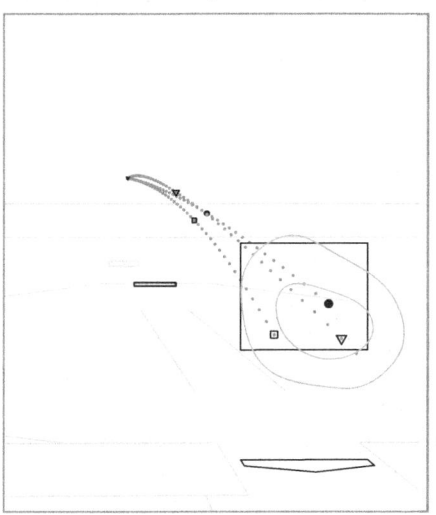

Type	Frequency	Velocity	H Movement	V Movement
● Fastball	56.7%	96.4 [112]	-3.6 [114]	-13.7 [106]
☐ Sinker	16.2%	96.7 [121]	-12.9 [98]	-18.6 [106]
+ Cutter				
▲ Changeup	1.3%	89.2 [115]	-11 [101]	-27.7 [99]
✕ Splitter				
▽ Slider	25.8%	81.9 [89]	16.4 [150]	-38.7 [83]
◇ Curveball				
✦ Slow Curveball				
✱ Knuckleball				
▼ Screwball				

Michael Feliz RHP

Born: 06/28/93   Age: 26   Bats: R   Throws: R
Height: 6'4"   Weight: 230   Origin: International Free Agent, 2010

YEAR	TEAM	LVL	AGE	W	L	SV	G	GS	IP	H	HR	BB/9	K/9	K	GB%	BABIP
2016	FRE	AAA	23	1	0	0	2	2	8¹	8	1	7.6	7.6	7	44%	.292
2016	HOU	MLB	23	8	1	0	47	0	65	55	10	3.0	13.2	95	42%	.315
2017	HOU	MLB	24	4	2	0	46	0	48	53	8	4.1	13.1	70	31%	.381
2018	IND	AAA	25	2	1	2	9	0	10	13	2	0.9	10.8	12	40%	.393
2018	PIT	MLB	25	1	2	0	47	0	47²	49	6	4.3	10.4	55	33%	.331
2019	PIT	MLB	26	2	2	0	41	0	43	40	5	3.8	10.1	49	38%	.301

Breakout: 31%   Improve: 49%   Collapse: 9%   Attrition: 14%   MLB: 82%
Comparables: Hong-Chih Kuo, Fernando Cabrera, Jensen Lewis

"Closer stuff." Even in the metrics-driven world of 2018, this is still shorthand for a high relief ceiling. Feliz has been tagged with this label ever since he was a teenager in the Astros' system. The problem is that while his raw stuff is drool-worthy, he is consistently inconsistent. Feliz's slider is a wipeout pitch, but when he can't throw it for strikes, hitters simply wait for ball four or a meaty fastball. His inaugural season as a Pirate was a lost one, and he has now struggled with his command/consistency for a season and a half. He has the talent to turn it around, but this can be said for any of the gazillion relievers on the cusp of a big-league roster with one superb pitch.

YEAR	TEAM	LVL	AGE	WHIP	ERA	DRA	WARP	MPH	FB%	WHF	CSP
2016	FRE	AAA	23	1.80	9.72	4.20	0.1				
2016	HOU	MLB	23	1.18	4.43	2.44	1.9	98.1	63.3	14.5	46.2
2017	HOU	MLB	24	1.56	5.62	3.18	1.1	98.1	71.9	15.4	50.4
2018	IND	AAA	25	1.40	7.20	2.74	0.3				
2018	PIT	MLB	25	1.51	5.66	5.20	-0.1	97.0	73.6	11	46.1
2019	PIT	MLB	26	1.34	3.97	4.28	0.3	97.3	71.3	13.6	48.4

Michael Feliz, continued

Pitch Shape vs LHH

Pitch Shape vs RHH

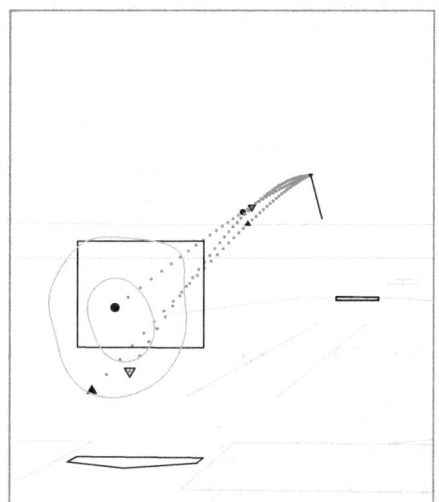 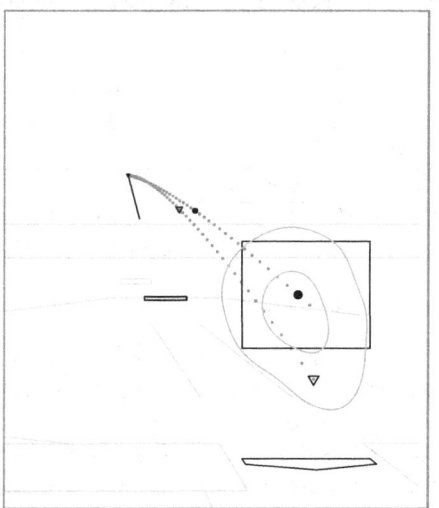

Type	Frequency	Velocity	H Movement	V Movement
● Fastball	71.5%	95.5 [110]	-2.3 [120]	-11.2 [114]
□ Sinker	2.0%	94.1 [108]	-9.4 [126]	-14.5 [119]
+ Cutter				
▲ Changeup	4.7%	88.4 [112]	-8.1 [117]	-22.2 [115]
× Splitter				
▽ Slider	21.7%	83.9 [98]	5.2 [101]	-30.9 [106]
◇ Curveball				
⊕ Slow Curveball				
✳ Knuckleball				
▼ Screwball				

Clay Holmes   RHP

Born: 03/27/93   Age: 26   Bats: R   Throws: R
Height: 6'5"   Weight: 230   Origin: Round 9, 2011 Draft (#272 overall)

YEAR	TEAM	LVL	AGE	W	L	SV	G	GS	IP	H	HR	BB/9	K/9	K	GB%	BABIP
2016	ALT	AA	23	10	9	0	26	26	136^1	138	10	4.2	6.7	101	63%	.314
2017	IND	AAA	24	10	5	0	25	24	112^2	96	4	4.7	7.9	99	62%	.302
2018	BRD	A+	25	0	0	0	1	1	6	4	0	0.0	12.0	8	79%	.286
2018	IND	AAA	25	8	3	0	22	16	95^1	94	4	3.8	9.4	100	61%	.346
2018	PIT	MLB	25	1	3	0	11	4	26^1	30	2	7.9	7.2	21	58%	.346
2019	PIT	MLB	26	3	3	0	23	8	56^1	53	4	4.5	8.2	51	56%	.301

Breakout: 18%   Improve: 29%   Collapse: 19%   Attrition: 27%   MLB: 55%
Comparables: Jesse Biddle, Dallas Beeler, Jimmy Nelson

(exasperated sigh)

   "How many times do I have to go through this? My name is Clay Holmes. I am a pitching prospect for the Pittsburgh Pirates. I made my major-league debut in 2018. The Pirates primarily used me as a reliever, although I started three times. I throw baseballs, not stones. The baseballs I throw can touch 99 mph, although it is more common for them to travel in the mid-90s. I sometimes have difficulty controlling those baseballs and hand out a lot of walks when that happens. My future is most likely going to be as a reliever, hopefully in a major-league bullpen. But your joke about 'people in glass houses shouldn't throw stones' is idiotic. My name isn't Glass Houses. It's Clay Holmes. And even if my name were 'Glass Houses,' I'd be the glass house, not the person inside of the glass house throwing stones. Your joke would work if there were little people inside me controlling everything I say and do, just like there were for Herman Brooks, the beloved title character in the witty yet short-lived early 1990s sitcom *Herman's Head*. Otherwise, your attempt at cheap humor at the expense of my perfectly NORMAL NAME simply doesn't make any sense."

YEAR	TEAM	LVL	AGE	WHIP	ERA	DRA	WARP	MPH	FB%	WHF	CSP
2016	ALT	AA	23	1.48	4.22	3.80	2.1				
2017	IND	AAA	24	1.38	3.36	4.51	1.5				
2018	BRD	A+	25	0.67	1.50	1.44	0.3				
2018	IND	AAA	25	1.41	3.40	5.05	0.5				
2018	PIT	MLB	25	2.01	6.84	6.25	-0.3	97.2	70.1	7.8	43.3
2019	PIT	MLB	26	1.47	4.08	4.43	0.4	96.8	71.4	8	44

Clay Holmes, continued

Pitch Shape vs LHH

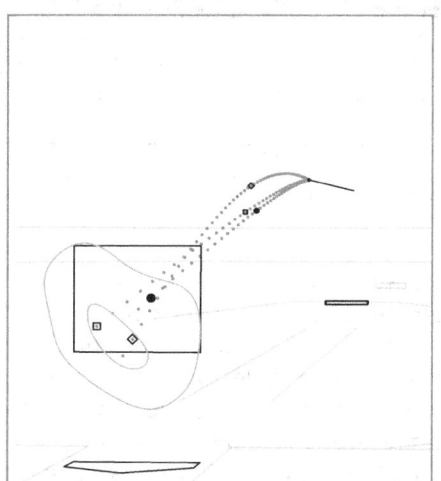

Pitch Shape vs RHH

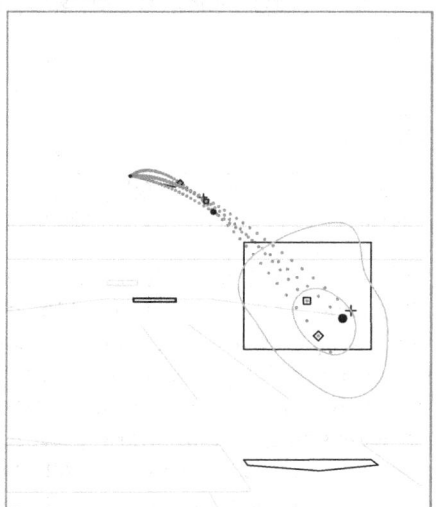

Type	Frequency	Velocity	H Movement	V Movement
● Fastball	23.4%	95 [108]	-7.5 [96]	-16.2 [99]
☐ Sinker	46.7%	94.7 [111]	-12.8 [98]	-21.7 [96]
+ Cutter	12.0%	89.9 [107]	1.1 [96]	-25.7 [92]
▲ Changeup	4.2%	87.8 [110]	-10.4 [105]	-28 [98]
✕ Splitter				
▽ Slider				
◇ Curveball	13.6%	81.9 [113]	6.9 [96]	-46.8 [103]
⊕ Slow Curveball				
✳ Knuckleball				
▼ Screwball				

Keone Kela RHP
Born: 04/16/93   Age: 26   Bats: R   Throws: R
Height: 6'1"   Weight: 215   Origin: Round 12, 2012 Draft (#396 overall)

YEAR	TEAM	LVL	AGE	W	L	SV	G	GS	IP	H	HR	BB/9	K/9	K	GB%	BABIP
2016	TEX	MLB	23	5	1	0	35	0	34	30	6	4.5	11.9	45	46%	.304
2017	TEX	MLB	24	4	1	2	39	0	38^2	18	4	4.0	11.9	51	32%	.179
2018	TEX	MLB	25	3	3	24	38	0	36^2	28	3	3.4	10.8	44	40%	.275
2018	PIT	MLB	25	0	1	0	16	0	15^1	10	2	2.9	12.9	22	27%	.258
2019	PIT	MLB	26	3	3	4	57	0	59	49	7	3.9	10.9	72	40%	.292

Breakout: 29%   Improve: 55%   Collapse: 20%   Attrition: 7%   MLB: 93%
Comparables: Corey Knebel, Rex Brothers, Ken Giles

It took far longer than anticipated, but Kela ascended to the top of the Rangers' bullpen and took over as closer at the beginning of 2018. As is the case with many young stoppers, Kela failed to make it through the year as closer, but in his case it wasn't injury or ineffectiveness but rather a trade that removed him from the role. Kela picked up right where he left off after joining the Pirates but was never going to supplant Felipe Vazquez regardless of how either hurler performed. Kela is almost exclusively a two-pitch pitcher but it's his hard, biting curveball that makes him so devastating, especially against right-handers. Pittsburgh shut Kela down due to "workload concerns" in September, but he is expected to be ready to answer the bell on Opening Day.

YEAR	TEAM	LVL	AGE	WHIP	ERA	DRA	WARP	MPH	FB%	WHF	CSP
2016	TEX	MLB	23	1.38	6.09	4.33	0.3	98.0	62.2	12.9	47.1
2017	TEX	MLB	24	0.91	2.79	4.75	0.2	98.2	57.9	12.2	49.6
2018	TEX	MLB	25	1.15	3.44	3.50	0.6	98.5	64.3	12.7	49.5
2018	PIT	MLB	25	0.98	2.93	2.37	0.5	98.2	58.7	16.1	50.3
2019	PIT	MLB	26	1.25	3.48	3.89	0.6	97.9	62.4	13.3	49.9

Keone Kela, continued

Pitch Shape vs LHH

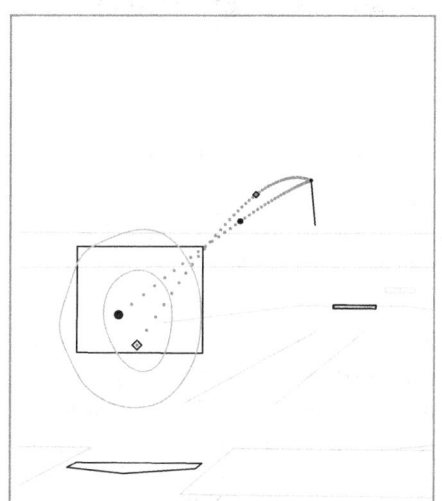

Pitch Shape vs RHH

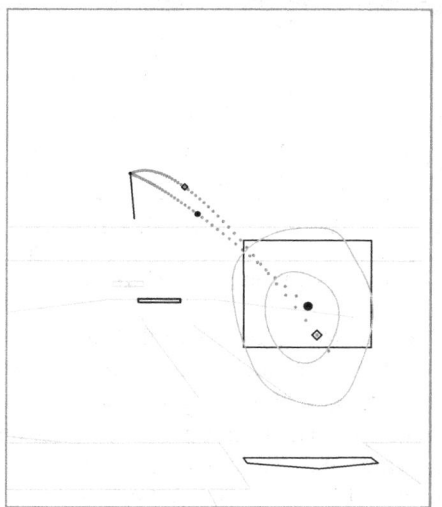

Type	Frequency	Velocity	H Movement	V Movement
● Fastball	62.8%	97.4 [116]	-1.3 [125]	-9.8 [119]
□ Sinker				
+ Cutter				
▲ Changeup	1.5%	91.7 [125]	-7.7 [119]	-17 [131]
✕ Splitter				
▽ Slider				
◇ Curveball	35.7%	83.6 [119]	2.4 [77]	-40.5 [117]
⊕ Slow Curveball				
✳ Knuckleball				
▼ Screwball				

Nick Kingham RHP

Born: 11/08/91 Age: 27 Bats: R Throws: R
Height: 6'5" Weight: 225 Origin: Round 4, 2010 Draft (#117 overall)

YEAR	TEAM	LVL	AGE	W	L	SV	G	GS	IP	H	HR	BB/9	K/9	K	GB%	BABIP
2016	PIR	RK	24	0	4	0	6	6	24	23	0	0.4	6.0	16	46%	.291
2016	BRD	A+	24	2	0	0	2	2	11	8	0	0.8	8.2	10	68%	.286
2016	ALT	AA	24	1	1	0	2	2	11	6	1	3.3	8.2	10	48%	.179
2017	IND	AAA	25	9	6	0	20	19	113^1	119	8	2.3	7.4	93	46%	.324
2018	IND	AAA	26	4	2	0	12	12	62^1	57	5	2.3	8.4	58	42%	.301
2018	PIT	MLB	26	5	7	0	18	15	76	79	18	3.1	8.2	69	40%	.272
2019	PIT	MLB	27	7	8	0	34	19	117	112	15	2.8	7.8	102	43%	.288

Breakout: 19% Improve: 29% Collapse: 22% Attrition: 32% MLB: 70%
Comparables: Albert Suarez, Mark Leiter, Kyle Lobstein

Success stories are uplifting, but often inure us to the fact that they're outliers. Kingham went under the knife for Tommy John surgery in 2015, struggled to make it back to the majors, and when he finally did arrive in 2018 his results were poor. The temptation is to write him off as a washout, but despite the lousy ERA and DRA, he showed some signs of life, a few positive indicators that could be a harbinger of hope. When he was on, Kingham commanded a low-90s fastball well on both sides of the plate, harnessed an excellent slider with a whiff rate over 20 percent and used his changeup as an out pitch to neutralize lefties. None of this sweeps his poor 2018 under the rug but reminds us that Kingham could eventually emerge as a no. 4 starter, and that injury recovery is art, not science.

YEAR	TEAM	LVL	AGE	WHIP	ERA	DRA	WARP	MPH	FB%	WHF	CSP
2016	PIR	RK	24	1.00	3.00	2.90	0.8				
2016	BRD	A+	24	0.82	0.00	4.18	0.2				
2016	ALT	AA	24	0.91	5.73	2.41	0.4				
2017	IND	AAA	25	1.31	4.13	3.91	2.2				
2018	IND	AAA	26	1.17	3.61	3.27	1.6				
2018	PIT	MLB	26	1.38	5.21	5.63	-0.3	93.9	56.4	11.8	46.4
2019	PIT	MLB	27	1.26	4.25	4.60	0.6	93.4	57.1	12	46.9

Nick Kingham, continued

Pitch Shape vs LHH

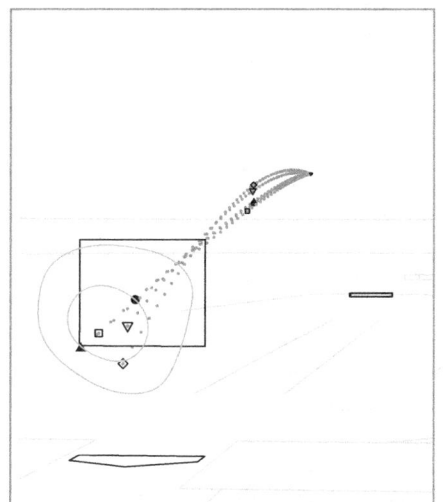

Pitch Shape vs RHH

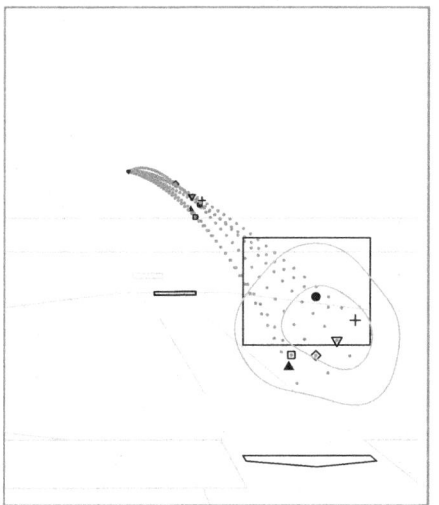

Type	Frequency	Velocity	H Movement	V Movement
● Fastball	40.4%	92.7 [101]	-3.6 [114]	-14.6 [104]
□ Sinker	16.0%	92.4 [100]	-11.8 [106]	-19.6 [102]
+ Cutter	7.4%	88.8 [100]	3.1 [107]	-24.2 [98]
▲ Changeup	15.3%	84.9 [98]	-13.8 [87]	-27.5 [99]
× Splitter				
▽ Slider	12.3%	84.5 [100]	2.3 [89]	-33 [100]
◇ Curveball	8.5%	80 [106]	6.6 [95]	-46.4 [104]
⊕ Slow Curveball				
✳ Knuckleball				
▼ Screwball				

Chad Kuhl RHP

Born: 09/10/92 Age: 26 Bats: R Throws: R
Height: 6'3" Weight: 216 Origin: Round 9, 2013 Draft (#269 overall)

YEAR	TEAM	LVL	AGE	W	L	SV	G	GS	IP	H	HR	BB/9	K/9	K	GB%	BABIP
2016	IND	AAA	23	6	3	0	16	16	83^2	81	9	1.7	7.1	66	48%	.295
2016	PIT	MLB	23	5	4	0	14	14	70^2	73	7	2.5	6.8	53	46%	.304
2017	PIT	MLB	24	8	11	0	31	31	157^1	159	17	4.1	8.1	142	43%	.321
2018	PIT	MLB	25	5	5	0	16	16	85	89	14	3.5	8.6	81	41%	.311
2019	PIT	MLB	26	5	5	0	16	16	83^2	77	9	3.2	8.6	80	43%	.309

Breakout: 37% Improve: 62% Collapse: 15% Attrition: 14% MLB: 91%
Comparables: Anthony DeSclafani, Mike Foltynewicz, Gavin Floyd

Ever since his major league debut in 2016, Kuhl looked a back-of-the-rotation arm, an innings eater who was unlikely to ever post an ERA under four. He was following the same script for most of 2018 until he started relying on his slider more and his heater less. For a brief period, Kuhl appeared to have shed that fifth-starter label, but a forearm strain in late June ended his season. Multiple attempts to get back on a mound led to additional pain and discomfort, and a medical exam in September led to a worst-case diagnosis and Tommy John surgery. Kuhl won't return until 2020. It's unknown what his recovery path will look like, and the Pirates have given no indications if they'll use an aggressive recovery path or keep Kuhl on ice.

YEAR	TEAM	LVL	AGE	WHIP	ERA	DRA	WARP	MPH	FB%	WHF	CSP
2016	IND	AAA	23	1.16	2.37	3.10	2.2				
2016	PIT	MLB	23	1.32	4.20	4.87	0.4	96.1	61.4	9.1	48.4
2017	PIT	MLB	24	1.47	4.35	5.35	0.4	97.8	63.5	10.3	47.7
2018	PIT	MLB	25	1.44	4.55	4.24	1.0	97.2	59	10.3	49.3
2019	PIT	MLB	26	1.28	3.89	4.47	0.8	96.9	62.8	10.3	49.4

Chad Kuhl, continued

Pitch Shape vs LHH

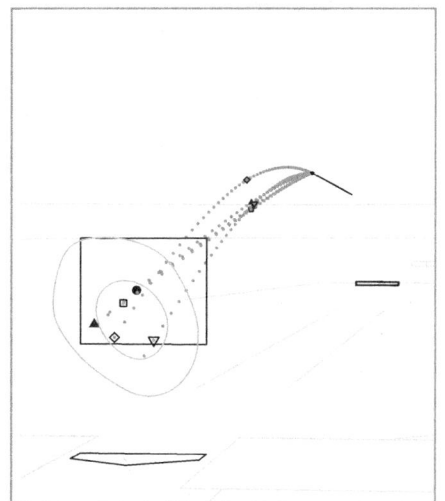

Pitch Shape vs RHH

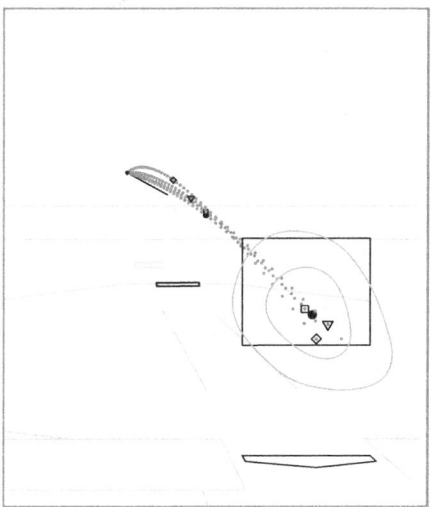

Type	Frequency	Velocity	H Movement	V Movement
● Fastball	12.8%	96.3 [112]	-9.4 [88]	-12.5 [110]
☐ Sinker	46.2%	95.9 [117]	-12 [105]	-14.4 [119]
+ Cutter				
▲ Changeup	8.1%	90.4 [120]	-13.1 [90]	-23.2 [112]
✕ Splitter				
▽ Slider	19.7%	88.7 [119]	4.9 [100]	-29.3 [111]
◇ Curveball	13.2%	83 [117]	9.3 [106]	-45.6 [105]
⊕ Slow Curveball				
✳ Knuckleball				
▼ Screwball				

Francisco Liriano LHP

Born: 10/26/83 Age: 35 Bats: L Throws: L
Height: 6'3" Weight: 218 Origin: International Free Agent, 2000

YEAR	TEAM	LVL	AGE	W	L	SV	G	GS	IP	H	HR	BB/9	K/9	K	GB%	BABIP
2016	PIT	MLB	32	6	11	0	21	21	113^2	115	19	5.5	9.2	116	54%	.308
2016	TOR	MLB	32	2	2	0	10	8	49^1	42	7	2.9	9.5	52	52%	.267
2017	TOR	MLB	33	6	5	0	18	18	82^2	91	11	4.7	8.1	74	44%	.327
2017	HOU	MLB	33	0	2	0	20	0	14^1	14	0	6.3	6.9	11	54%	.341
2018	DET	MLB	34	5	12	0	27	26	133^2	127	19	4.9	7.4	110	49%	.285
2019	PIT	MLB	35	7	8	0	22	22	117^2	111	13	4.5	8.3	108	48%	.308

Breakout: 10%   Improve: 34%   Collapse: 29%   Attrition: 14%   MLB: 86%
Comparables: Doug Davis, Ryan Dempster, A.J. Burnett

Liriano was once considered the top pitcher in baseball. That was 13 years ago, a unit of time longer than Sandy Koufax's entire career. Durability is a blessing and a curse; not everyone gets to pitch into a second decade. However, watching the 35-year-old Liriano gallivant about the circuit as a reduced shell of his electric rookie self is highly bittersweet. His attempt to reunite with Ron Gardenhire in Detroit to catalyze that 2006 magic brought us to the conclusion that it's not about location (although it is, in the other definition), he just can't retire righties. His last chance to provide meaningful outs is one at a time, as he did in the 2017 World Series, against lefties. (Both appearances were exclusively against Cody Bellinger, and he doesn't have to be that hyper-specialized, although Bellinger was 11 when Liriano was the talk of the league, and he would have struck him out then too.)

YEAR	TEAM	LVL	AGE	WHIP	ERA	DRA	WARP	MPH	FB%	WHF	CSP
2016	PIT	MLB	32	1.62	5.46	5.07	0.4	95.5	50.9	11.7	41.6
2016	TOR	MLB	32	1.18	2.92	4.77	0.3	95.9	51.1	13.1	42.3
2017	TOR	MLB	33	1.62	5.88	5.75	-0.2	94.5	49.3	10.1	42.2
2017	HOU	MLB	33	1.67	4.40	6.59	-0.2	96.1	54.6	10	44
2018	DET	MLB	34	1.50	4.58	5.36	-0.1	94.0	46.7	10.5	43.8
2019	PIT	MLB	35	1.44	4.37	5.02	0.4	93.5	48	10.7	42.1

Francisco Liriano, continued

Pitch Shape vs LHH

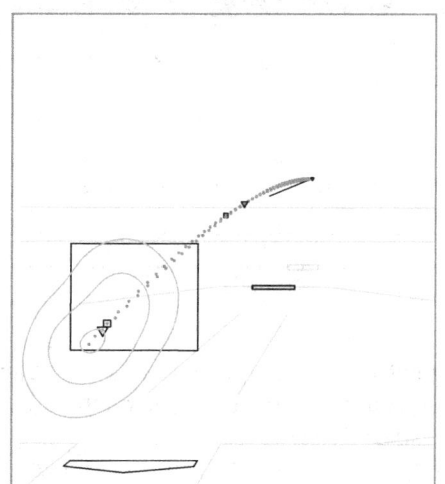

Pitch Shape vs RHH

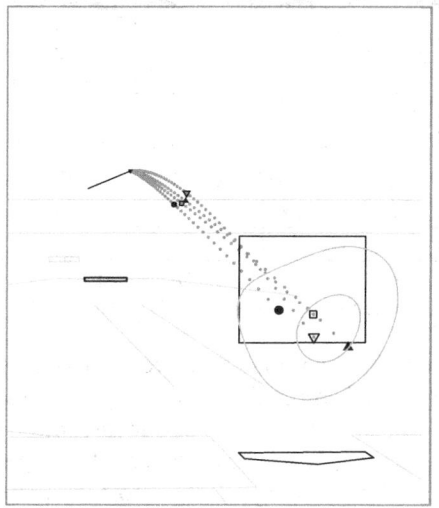

Type	Frequency	Velocity	H Movement	V Movement
● Fastball	3.8%	92.3 [99]	8.5 [92]	-16.4 [98]
☐ Sinker	42.9%	92.6 [100]	12.6 [100]	-19.1 [104]
+ Cutter				
▲ Changeup	20.1%	85.9 [102]	13.9 [86]	-28.1 [98]
✕ Splitter				
▽ Slider	33.1%	85 [103]	-1.9 [87]	-29.9 [109]
◇ Curveball	0.2%	76.5 [93]	-7.2 [97]	-45.9 [105]
✣ Slow Curveball				
✱ Knuckleball				
▼ Screwball				

Jordan Lyles   RHP

Born: 10/19/90   Age: 28   Bats: R   Throws: R
Height: 6'4"   Weight: 230   Origin: Round 1, 2008 Draft (#38 overall)

YEAR	TEAM	LVL	AGE	W	L	SV	G	GS	IP	H	HR	BB/9	K/9	K	GB%	BABIP
2016	ABQ	AAA	25	4	2	0	8	8	44^2	57	5	3.6	5.8	29	42%	.361
2016	COL	MLB	25	4	5	1	40	5	58^2	69	4	4.3	4.9	32	52%	.319
2017	COL	MLB	26	0	2	0	33	0	46^2	61	11	2.3	6.4	33	52%	.331
2017	ELP	AAA	26	1	1	0	5	5	20	20	1	3.6	9.0	20	48%	.333
2017	SDN	MLB	26	1	3	0	5	5	23	35	5	3.9	8.6	22	46%	.395
2018	SDN	MLB	27	2	4	0	24	8	71^1	71	12	2.4	7.8	62	47%	.286
2018	MIL	MLB	27	1	0	0	11	0	16^1	12	0	5.0	12.1	22	42%	.316
2019	PIT	MLB	28	4	5	0	49	8	83	83	10	3.5	7.9	74	46%	.300

Breakout: 17%   Improve: 52%   Collapse: 14%   Attrition: 16%   MLB: 91%
Comparables: Wily Peralta, Paul Maholm, Ivan Nova

Induced demand is the dream of both regulators and pitching coaches. In public policy, if you wish for folks to drive less frequently in the future, you might not write any regulations about cars, but instead design land-use policies encouraging dense housing without parking spots. In coaching, if you hope to rehab a scuffling pitcher into a strikeout machine, you might not make any adjustment to his fastball, instead opting to shuffle those secondaries. Such is the case with Lyles, a middling, five-pitch journeyman who struck out 14 percent of batters faced in Colorado and 20 percent in San Diego. As soon as Lyles came to Milwaukee, the curveball became his primary pitch, but the extra whiffs didn't occur with the breaking ball. By simplifying Lyles' approach and placing focus on the fastball and curve, the whiffs on the fastball suddenly began piling up. This creates a new decision tree for the veteran, who can further induce those strikeouts by doubling down on simple two-pitch approach, or now slowly tinker with his other pitches to refine his starting value.

YEAR	TEAM	LVL	AGE	WHIP	ERA	DRA	WARP	MPH	FB%	WHF	CSP
2016	ABQ	AAA	25	1.68	5.44	4.73	0.3				
2016	COL	MLB	25	1.65	5.83	7.64	-1.7	95.7	59.3	8.3	45.7
2017	COL	MLB	26	1.56	6.94	5.61	-0.2	96.1	56.7	10.1	48.5
2017	ELP	AAA	26	1.40	4.50	3.10	0.6				
2017	SDN	MLB	26	1.96	9.39	4.14	0.3	94.5	53.3	10.9	43.3
2018	SDN	MLB	27	1.26	4.29	5.91	-0.6	95.6	48.8	10.2	50.2
2018	MIL	MLB	27	1.29	3.31	2.57	0.5	96.1	47.6	14.5	46.6
2019	PIT	MLB	28	1.39	4.38	4.67	0.2	95.1	53.2	10.3	47.9

Jordan Lyles, continued

Pitch Shape vs LHH

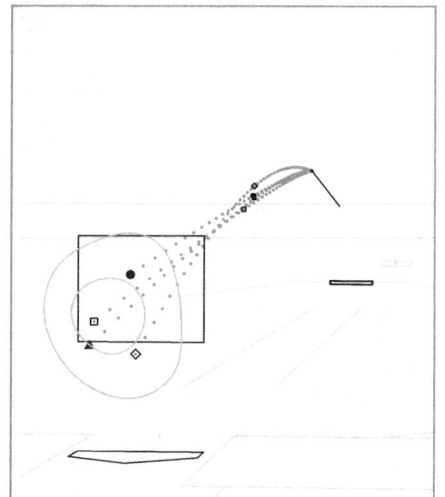

Pitch Shape vs RHH

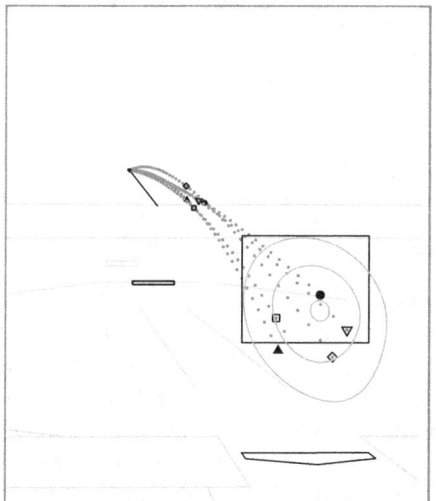

Type		Frequency	Velocity	H Movement	V Movement
●	Fastball	35.6%	94.6 [107]	-7.4 [97]	-13.4 [107]
☐	Sinker	12.9%	93.8 [106]	-12.8 [98]	-18.3 [107]
+	Cutter				
▲	Changeup	13.1%	86.6 [105]	-12.8 [92]	-28.9 [95]
✕	Splitter				
▽	Slider	9.6%	89.8 [124]	3.4 [94]	-25.1 [123]
◇	Curveball	28.8%	84.2 [121]	4.5 [86]	-45.3 [106]
✦	Slow Curveball				
✳	Knuckleball				
▼	Screwball				

Brandon Maurer   RHP

Born: 07/03/90   Age: 28   Bats: R   Throws: R
Height: 6'5"   Weight: 225   Origin: Round 23, 2008 Draft (#702 overall)

YEAR	TEAM	LVL	AGE	W	L	SV	G	GS	IP	H	HR	BB/9	K/9	K	GB%	BABIP
2016	SDN	MLB	25	0	5	13	71	0	69^2	65	7	3.0	9.3	72	39%	.297
2017	SDN	MLB	26	1	4	20	42	0	39^1	39	4	1.8	8.7	38	44%	.315
2017	KCA	MLB	26	2	2	2	26	0	20	34	4	4.9	9.4	21	33%	.435
2018	OMA	AAA	27	1	3	5	19	0	23	23	1	5.1	9.4	24	54%	.333
2018	KCA	MLB	27	0	4	1	37	0	31^1	42	7	7.2	8.9	31	43%	.365
2019	PIT	MLB	28	3	1	8	51	0	54	51	5	4.0	8.7	52	42%	.315

Breakout: 25%   Improve: 54%   Collapse: 17%   Attrition: 5%   MLB: 95%
Comparables: Mark Lowe, Dan Wheeler, Tony Castillo

When mysteries are presented to the human mind, we will always speculate as to their answers, even in the absence of sufficient data or evidence. The mystery of Maurer's silent "r" is no different. The Padres, noting Maurer's spotty record as a starter, took it to stand for "reliever," and he became a usable closer over parts of two seasons. Kansas City may have interpreted it to mean "Royal," and they acquired him in a six-player deadline deal in 2017. Once in KC, the mystery of the silent "r" was solved beyond any doubt: it stood for "runs," of which Maurer gave up nearly one per inning in his two-season tenure. The Royals had the literal last "r" word, however, releasing the disappointing righty after the 2018 season.

YEAR	TEAM	LVL	AGE	WHIP	ERA	DRA	WARP	MPH	FB%	WHF	CSP
2016	SDN	MLB	25	1.26	4.52	3.80	0.9	98.4	55.3	12.7	48.4
2017	SDN	MLB	26	1.19	5.72	4.61	0.2	98.6	58.2	11	52
2017	KCA	MLB	26	2.25	8.10	5.27	0.0	98.8	54.6	10.6	50
2018	OMA	AAA	27	1.57	5.48	2.61	0.7				
2018	KCA	MLB	27	2.14	7.76	6.45	-0.5	98.7	44.3	11	46
2019	PIT	MLB	28	1.40	4.01	4.62	0.2	98.0	52.8	11.5	48.6

Brandon Maurer, continued

Pitch Shape vs LHH

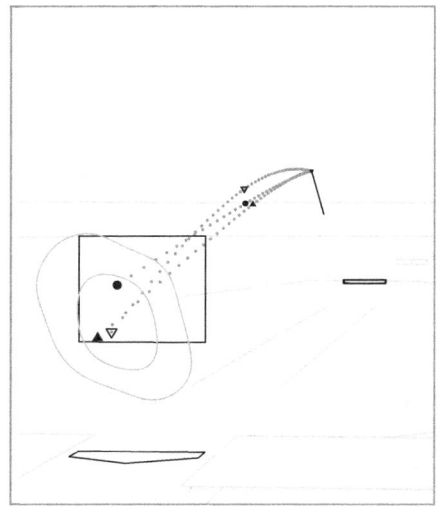

Pitch Shape vs RHH

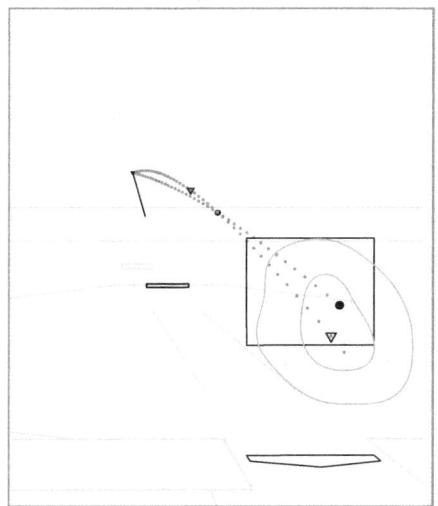

Type	Frequency	Velocity	H Movement	V Movement
● Fastball	39.9%	96.5 [113]	-7.5 [96]	-11.5 [113]
☐ Sinker	4.4%	95.4 [115]	-13.5 [92]	-18.9 [105]
+ Cutter				
▲ Changeup	13.2%	87.4 [108]	-12.2 [95]	-23.8 [111]
✕ Splitter				
▽ Slider	42.5%	85.4 [104]	5.2 [102]	-38.1 [85]
◇ Curveball				
✣ Slow Curveball				
✶ Knuckleball				
▼ Screwball				

Pittsburgh Pirates 2019

Joe Musgrove RHP

Born: 12/04/92   Age: 26   Bats: R   Throws: R
Height: 6'5"   Weight: 260   Origin: Round 1, 2011 Draft (#46 overall)

YEAR	TEAM	LVL	AGE	W	L	SV	G	GS	IP	H	HR	BB/9	K/9	K	GB%	BABIP
2016	CCH	AA	23	2	1	0	6	4	26^1	19	1	1.0	10.3	30	49%	.265
2016	FRE	AAA	23	5	3	0	10	10	59	60	8	1.1	8.7	57	55%	.317
2016	HOU	MLB	23	4	4	0	11	10	62	59	9	2.3	8.0	55	43%	.289
2017	FRE	AAA	24	1	0	0	1	1	7	1	0	2.6	9.0	7	54%	.077
2017	HOU	MLB	24	7	8	2	38	15	109^1	117	18	2.3	8.1	98	46%	.316
2018	IND	AAA	25	1	1	0	2	2	10^2	10	0	1.7	9.3	11	41%	.312
2018	PIT	MLB	25	6	9	0	19	19	115^1	113	12	1.8	7.8	100	48%	.294
2019	PIT	MLB	26	8	8	0	24	24	136	129	16	2.4	8.4	127	46%	.292

Breakout: 32%   Improve: 55%   Collapse: 16%   Attrition: 4%   MLB: 93%
Comparables: Patrick Corbin, Jordan Zimmermann, Jake Odorizzi

If you're reading this chapter beginning-to-end, you're probably tired of hearing about Gerrit Cole, especially if you're a Pirates fan. That's right, Musgrove was part of the four-player package Pittsburgh received in exchange for their young, cost-controlled ace. When he was able to take the hill, Musgrove put together a solid season. He increased his use of a cutter he picked up from former major leaguer Jerome Williams in 2016, relying less on his slider and dropping his curve almost entirely. Musgrove's DRA was a notable improvement over his previous seasons, but the problem was he couldn't stay on the mound. The big right-hander missed time due to a shoulder strain, a finger infection and an abdominal strain. There's more ceiling here than the naysayers expected when the Pirates acquired Musgrove, but he'll need to stay healthy for a full season for that potential to be realized.

YEAR	TEAM	LVL	AGE	WHIP	ERA	DRA	WARP	MPH	FB%	WHF	CSP
2016	CCH	AA	23	0.84	0.34	2.44	0.8				
2016	FRE	AAA	23	1.14	3.81	2.82	1.7				
2016	HOU	MLB	23	1.21	4.06	4.43	0.6	94.6	45.6	10.4	48.7
2017	FRE	AAA	24	0.43	0.00	3.52	0.2				
2017	HOU	MLB	24	1.33	4.77	4.49	1.2	95.7	48	13	51.6
2018	IND	AAA	25	1.12	5.06	3.41	0.3				
2018	PIT	MLB	25	1.18	4.06	3.43	2.5	95.0	50.3	12.5	53.5
2019	PIT	MLB	26	1.20	3.81	4.14	1.5	94.8	49.5	12.6	52.6

Joe Musgrove, continued

Pitch Shape vs LHH

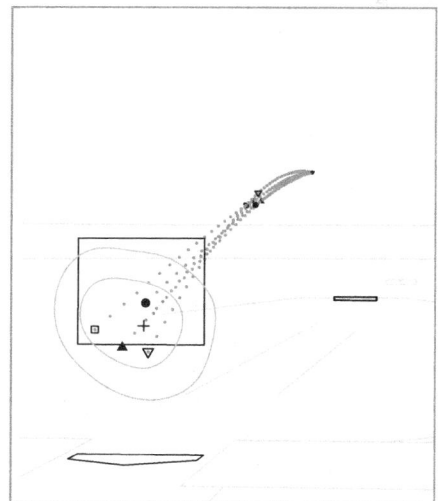

Pitch Shape vs RHH

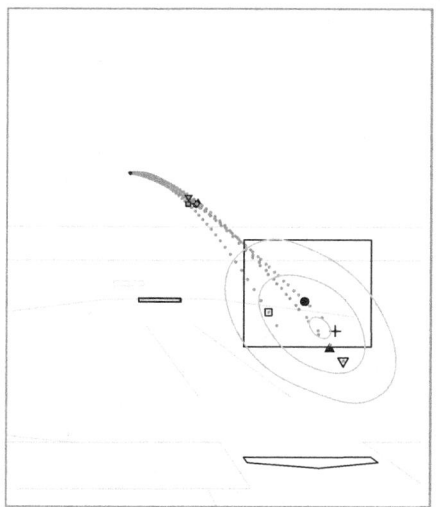

Type		Frequency	Velocity	H Movement	V Movement
●	Fastball	33.2%	94 [105]	-3.5 [115]	-15.9 [99]
□	Sinker	17.1%	92.5 [100]	-8.9 [131]	-22.8 [92]
+	Cutter	15.0%	89.8 [106]	3.4 [109]	-23.7 [100]
▲	Changeup	13.9%	85.9 [102]	-8 [117]	-28.2 [98]
×	Splitter				
▽	Slider	20.2%	84.3 [99]	5.9 [104]	-36.2 [91]
◇	Curveball	0.5%	80.9 [109]	7.2 [97]	-47.7 [101]
✥	Slow Curveball				
✱	Knuckleball				
▼	Screwball				

Pittsburgh Pirates 2019

Richard Rodriguez RHP
Born: 03/04/90 Age: 29 Bats: R Throws: R
Height: 6'4" Weight: 205 Origin: International Free Agent, 2010

YEAR	TEAM	LVL	AGE	W	L	SV	G	GS	IP	H	HR	BB/9	K/9	K	GB%	BABIP
2016	NOR	AAA	26	6	2	2	48	2	81^2	65	5	2.8	8.9	81	34%	.276
2017	NOR	AAA	27	4	4	10	42	1	70^2	56	5	2.3	10.2	80	29%	.285
2017	BAL	MLB	27	0	0	0	5	0	5^2	12	4	4.8	4.8	3	46%	.400
2018	PIT	MLB	28	4	3	0	63	0	69^1	55	5	2.5	11.4	88	40%	.309
2019	PIT	MLB	29	3	2	0	51	0	54	46	6	3.3	10.0	61	37%	.291

Breakout: 7% Improve: 18% Collapse: 29% Attrition: 31% MLB: 54%
Comparables: Miguel Socolovich, Justin Miller, Spencer Patton

An anonymous minor-league journeyman who looked like he was one-and-done in the majors after an awful Orioles stint in 2017, Rodriguez not only survived in his new Pittsburgh home; he thrived. Rodriguez throws a decent enough fastball and slider, but his success came thanks to a newfound ability with location that would make Cookie Kwan envious. Only seven relievers (minimum 50 IP) threw more strikes in the zone than Rodriguez, but despite this, he ranked in the bottom third on contact for pitches in the zone as a result of improved command. Late-blooming relievers are sometimes one-year wonders, but Rodriguez's Days of Obligation working his way up to the majors are probably over, and he'll rely on the Hunger of Memory as inspiration to avoid getting demoted. Richard Rodriguez, autobiographical author and Emmy and Peabody Award winner? Nothing? Doesn't anyone listen to NPR anymore?

YEAR	TEAM	LVL	AGE	WHIP	ERA	DRA	WARP	MPH	FB%	WHF	CSP
2016	NOR	AAA	26	1.10	2.53	3.10	1.8				
2017	NOR	AAA	27	1.05	2.42	2.79	2.0				
2017	BAL	MLB	27	2.65	14.29	8.32	-0.2	95.3	65.8	6.7	50.2
2018	PIT	MLB	28	1.07	2.47	2.82	1.7	94.4	75.1	15.2	50.7
2019	PIT	MLB	29	1.22	3.69	4.06	0.5	93.8	74.3	14.5	50.5

Richard Rodriguez, continued

Pitch Shape vs LHH

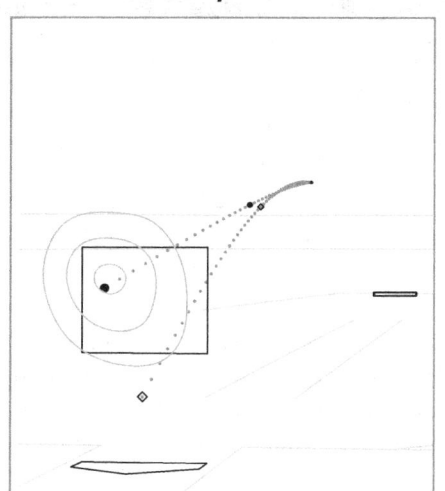

Pitch Shape vs RHH

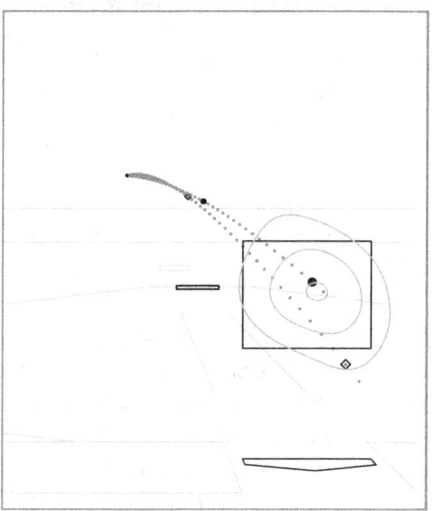

Type	Frequency	Velocity	H Movement	V Movement
● Fastball	75.1%	93.5 [103]	-10.2 [84]	-14.8 [103]
☐ Sinker				
+ Cutter				
▲ Changeup	0.1%	85.7 [101]	-7.3 [121]	-19.5 [123]
✕ Splitter				
▽ Slider				
◇ Curveball	24.8%	81.5 [111]	3.9 [83]	-40.3 [117]
⊕ Slow Curveball				
✱ Knuckleball				
▼ Screwball				

Pirates Player Analysis - 73

Edgar Santana RHP

Born: 10/16/91 Age: 27 Bats: R Throws: R
Height: 6'2" Weight: 195 Origin: International Free Agent, 2013

YEAR	TEAM	LVL	AGE	W	L	SV	G	GS	IP	H	HR	BB/9	K/9	K	GB%	BABIP
2016	BRD	A+	24	2	0	0	9	0	22[1]	13	0	0.8	8.1	20	61%	.220
2016	ALT	AA	24	2	1	2	21	0	41[1]	32	4	2.4	8.5	39	57%	.264
2016	IND	AAA	24	0	0	1	13	0	16	22	1	3.4	6.8	12	53%	.389
2017	IND	AAA	25	1	3	8	44	0	58	62	4	1.9	8.4	54	44%	.343
2017	PIT	MLB	25	0	0	0	19	0	18	16	2	6.0	10.0	20	46%	.304
2018	PIT	MLB	26	3	4	0	69	0	66[1]	61	7	1.6	7.3	54	47%	.277
2019	PIT	MLB	27	3	1	1	55	0	58	55	7	2.9	8.3	54	47%	.306

Breakout: 16% Improve: 28% Collapse: 28% Attrition: 30% MLB: 72%
Comparables: Donnie Hart, Nick Wittgren, Derek Law

Closers aren't born but rather invented, so when Felipe Vazquez complained of forearm discomfort in May, it appeared Santana might step into the ninth inning role for the Bucs. Vazquez's pain turned out to be much ado about nothing, so Santana quietly trudged along in a set-up role. He struggled in the first half but went through a 27.1-inning stretch in July and August where his tailing mid-90s fastball and mid-80s slider were almost unhittable. The wheels came off late in the season. Santana's strikeouts plummeted and after posting a 12.60 ERA in five miserable September innings, and an examination with Dr. James Andrews led to Tommy John surgery at the end of the season. Santana won't return until 2020.

YEAR	TEAM	LVL	AGE	WHIP	ERA	DRA	WARP	MPH	FB%	WHF	CSP
2016	BRD	A+	24	0.67	0.81	2.69	0.6				
2016	ALT	AA	24	1.04	2.83	3.17	0.8				
2016	IND	AAA	24	1.75	5.06	3.43	0.3				
2017	IND	AAA	25	1.28	2.79	3.24	1.3				
2017	PIT	MLB	25	1.56	3.50	4.47	0.1	96.7	61.2	15.2	46.2
2018	PIT	MLB	26	1.10	3.26	3.56	1.0	96.0	57.6	12.6	51.5
2019	PIT	MLB	27	1.27	4.09	4.70	0.2	95.6	59	13.3	49.7

Edgar Santana, continued

Pitch Shape vs LHH

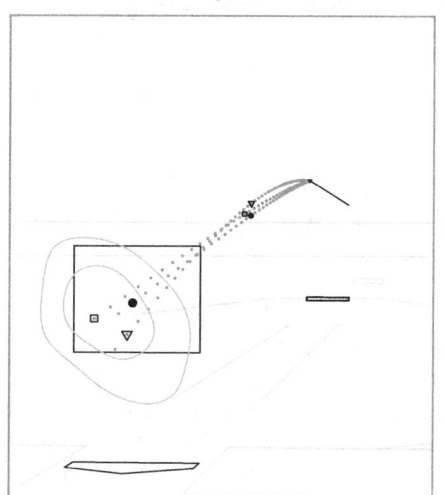

Pitch Shape vs RHH

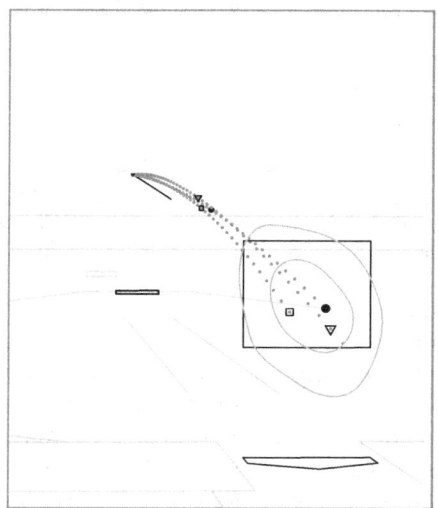

Type	Frequency	Velocity	H Movement	V Movement
● Fastball	17.9%	95.4 [109]	-10.1 [84]	-13.5 [107]
☐ Sinker	39.7%	95.1 [113]	-13.2 [95]	-16.9 [111]
+ Cutter				
▲ Changeup	2.3%	89.4 [116]	-9.7 [109]	-20.9 [119]
✕ Splitter				
▽ Slider	40.1%	87.3 [113]	-1.5 [72]	-30.9 [106]
◇ Curveball				
⊕ Slow Curveball				
✶ Knuckleball				
▼ Screwball				

Jameson Taillon RHP

Born: 11/18/91 Age: 27 Bats: R Throws: R
Height: 6'5" Weight: 230 Origin: Round 1, 2010 Draft (#2 overall)

YEAR	TEAM	LVL	AGE	W	L	SV	G	GS	IP	H	HR	BB/9	K/9	K	GB%	BABIP
2016	IND	AAA	24	4	2	0	10	10	61²	44	2	0.9	8.9	61	49%	.253
2016	PIT	MLB	24	5	4	0	18	18	104	99	13	1.5	7.4	85	55%	.287
2017	IND	AAA	25	0	1	0	2	2	11	12	0	1.6	12.3	15	58%	.387
2017	PIT	MLB	25	8	7	0	25	25	133²	152	11	3.1	8.4	125	49%	.352
2018	PIT	MLB	26	14	10	0	32	32	191	179	20	2.2	8.4	179	48%	.298
2019	PIT	MLB	27	11	10	0	30	30	180	166	17	2.4	8.6	171	48%	.296

Breakout: 21% Improve: 59% Collapse: 19% Attrition: 6% MLB: 96%
Comparables: Kevin Gausman, Patrick Corbin, Ricky Nolasco

Drafted as the second overall pick way back in 2010, Taillon has seen fellow first-rounders Chris Sale, Bryce Harper, Manny Machado and Christian Yelich blossom into superstars while he took a more methodical path to the majors. To be fair, pitchers drafted out of high school have a longer development cycle, but Taillon also took a detour down Tommy John Way in 2014 and survived testicular cancer in 2017. Nearly a decade after he was drafted, Taillon finally turned potential into a full season of high-end results. Taillon's 191 innings easily topped his career high. He added a 90-mph slider to his already devastating fastball-curve combo, resulting in a top-20 season by WARP. While it seems like he has been around forever, Taillon is only 27, and still young enough to be as much of a star as those other names who were part of his illustrious draft class.

YEAR	TEAM	LVL	AGE	WHIP	ERA	DRA	WARP	MPH	FB%	WHF	CSP
2016	IND	AAA	24	0.81	2.04	3.17	1.5				
2016	PIT	MLB	24	1.12	3.38	3.89	1.7	96.5	63.1	9.1	46.6
2017	IND	AAA	25	1.27	4.09	2.00	0.4				
2017	PIT	MLB	25	1.48	4.44	4.08	2.2	96.7	64.1	9.6	48
2018	PIT	MLB	26	1.18	3.20	3.41	4.2	96.7	57.3	11.8	48.6
2019	PIT	MLB	27	1.19	3.46	3.77	2.7	96.2	61.2	10.8	48.5

Jameson Taillon, continued

Pitch Shape vs LHH

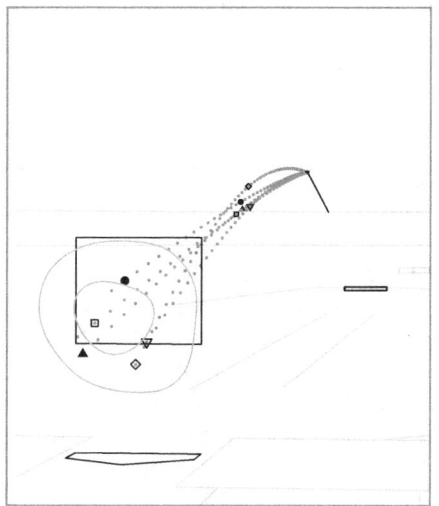

Pitch Shape vs RHH

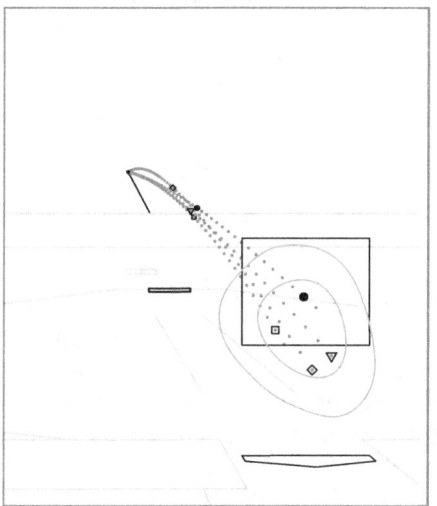

Type	Frequency	Velocity	H Movement	V Movement
● Fastball	35.2%	95.8 [111]	-3 [117]	-12.8 [109]
☐ Sinker	22.2%	95.8 [117]	-11.3 [110]	-17.1 [110]
+ Cutter				
▲ Changeup	4.6%	88.5 [113]	-7.6 [120]	-23 [113]
✕ Splitter				
▽ Slider	18.2%	90.2 [126]	4.5 [98]	-24.1 [126]
◇ Curveball	19.8%	82.8 [116]	9.8 [108]	-47.4 [102]
⊕ Slow Curveball				
✱ Knuckleball				
▼ Screwball				

Felipe Vazquez   LHP

Born: 07/05/91   Age: 27   Bats: L   Throws: L
Height: 6'2"   Weight: 210   Origin: International Free Agent, 2008

YEAR	TEAM	LVL	AGE	W	L	SV	G	GS	IP	H	HR	BB/9	K/9	K	GB%	BABIP
2016	WAS	MLB	24	0	3	1	47	0	49^2	43	4	2.7	9.6	53	48%	.310
2016	PIT	MLB	24	1	3	0	28	0	27^1	23	3	5.9	12.8	39	48%	.317
2017	PIT	MLB	25	5	3	21	73	0	75^1	47	4	2.4	10.5	88	53%	.234
2018	PIT	MLB	26	4	2	37	70	0	70	63	4	3.1	11.4	89	44%	.331
2019	PIT	MLB	27	3	3	34	57	0	59	49	6	3.4	10.5	70	46%	.293

Breakout: 24%   Improve: 50%   Collapse: 34%   Attrition: 8%   MLB: 99%
Comparables: Juan Rincon, Kelvin Herrera, Manny Delcarmen

In April 2018, he decided to legally change his surname from Rivero to Vazquez to honor his sister's influence on both his life and career. Shakespeare said that a rose by any other name smells just as sweet. In Vazquez's case, it didn't matter what he called himself because he kept delivering the same filth to batters that he had since becoming a Pirate in 2016. A case of forearm discomfort in May turned out to be nothing serious. The control issues that plagued him at the beginning of his Pirates' tenure are a memory, and health is the only thing potentially standing between Vazquez and a string of elite seasons at closer.

YEAR	TEAM	LVL	AGE	WHIP	ERA	DRA	WARP	MPH	FB%	WHF	CSP
2016	WAS	MLB	24	1.17	4.53	3.02	1.1	98.5	62.3	15.9	48.2
2016	PIT	MLB	24	1.50	3.29	2.96	0.6	99.8	61.1	15.8	47.7
2017	PIT	MLB	25	0.89	1.67	2.59	2.2	100.7	61	16.3	51.8
2018	PIT	MLB	26	1.24	2.70	2.64	1.8	100.5	65.6	15.8	53.8
2019	PIT	MLB	27	1.20	3.02	3.49	0.9	99.7	63.9	16.2	52.3

Felipe Vazquez, continued

Pitch Shape vs LHH

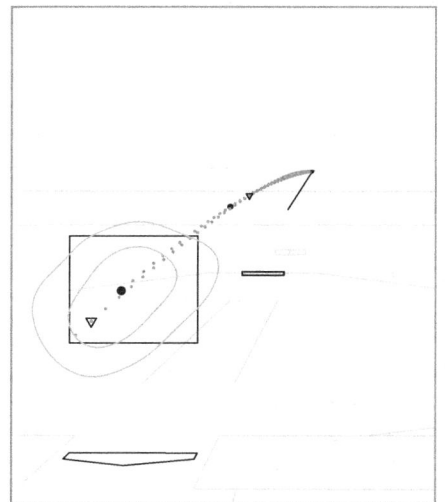

Pitch Shape vs RHH

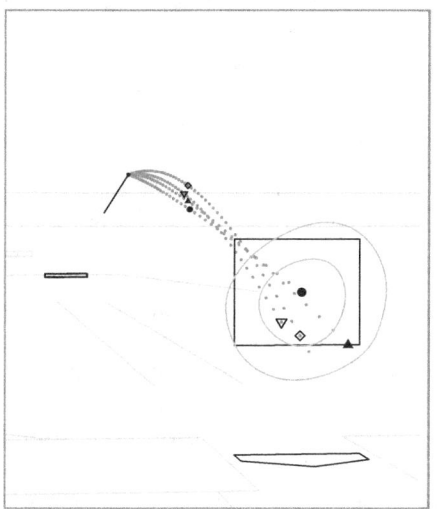

Type		Frequency	Velocity	H Movement	V Movement
●	Fastball	65.4%	98.5 [119]	8.5 [92]	-13.3 [108]
☐	Sinker	0.2%	99.2 [134]	15.1 [80]	-20.4 [100]
+	Cutter				
▲	Changeup	19.1%	89 [114]	12 [96]	-30.2 [91]
✕	Splitter				
▽	Slider	9.0%	86.8 [110]	-9.8 [121]	-29.1 [111]
◇	Curveball	6.4%	82 [113]	-10.1 [110]	-42.6 [112]
⊕	Slow Curveball				
✱	Knuckleball				
▼	Screwball				

Trevor Williams RHP
Born: 04/25/92   Age: 27   Bats: R   Throws: R
Height: 6'3"   Weight: 230   Origin: Round 2, 2013 Draft (#44 overall)

YEAR	TEAM	LVL	AGE	W	L	SV	G	GS	IP	H	HR	BB/9	K/9	K	GB%	BABIP
2016	IND	AAA	24	9	6	0	20	19	110^1	103	5	2.4	6.0	74	53%	.284
2016	PIT	MLB	24	1	1	0	7	1	12^2	19	4	3.6	7.8	11	49%	.366
2017	PIT	MLB	25	7	9	0	31	25	150^1	145	14	3.1	7.0	117	50%	.292
2018	PIT	MLB	26	14	10	0	31	31	170^2	146	15	2.9	6.6	126	43%	.261
2019	PIT	MLB	27	8	10	0	26	26	148	147	18	2.9	7.3	120	46%	.293

Breakout: 17%   Improve: 42%   Collapse: 18%   Attrition: 12%   MLB: 80%
Comparables: Sergio Mitre, Dillon Gee, Kyle Gibson

On July 6, Williams allowed five runs in 2 1/3 innings to the Philadelphia Phillies. His ERA jumped to 4.60, and he didn't appear to be long for the Pirates rotation. Williams turned his season around after that start, although saying he turned it around is like saying Abraham Lincoln gave a little speech in Gettysburg. In his last 13 starts, Williams posted a ridiculous 1.29 ERA, looking like a world beater in the process. An absurdly great strand rate was tabbed as the primary reason for Williams' good fortune, but it wasn't all a matter of random batted-ball luck. Williams' usual masterful command of all his pitches was on display, but he also started pitching lower in the zone, making it more difficult to lift any of his offerings, especially his sinker. It also helped that he took a little something off his slider, creating more separation between it and his fastball. The odds of another season with an ERA near three is as likely as Williams arriving to Spring Training tattoo-free, but the year wasn't an entire fluke. The former Sun Devil is a smart pitcher with a strong fastball who knows how to command everything else in order to maximize his otherwise average stuff.

YEAR	TEAM	LVL	AGE	WHIP	ERA	DRA	WARP	MPH	FB%	WHF	CSP
2016	IND	AAA	24	1.21	2.53	4.69	0.8				
2016	PIT	MLB	24	1.89	7.82	5.39	0.0	96.7	66.5	9.8	48.2
2017	PIT	MLB	25	1.31	4.07	4.49	1.8	94.6	71.6	9.1	46.4
2018	PIT	MLB	26	1.18	3.11	4.28	2.0	93.1	69.4	8.8	46
2019	PIT	MLB	27	1.31	4.24	4.61	0.8	93.3	71	9.1	47.3

Trevor Williams, continued

Pitch Shape vs LHH

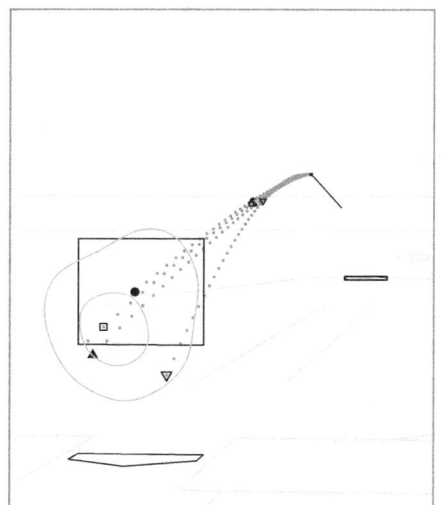

Pitch Shape vs RHH

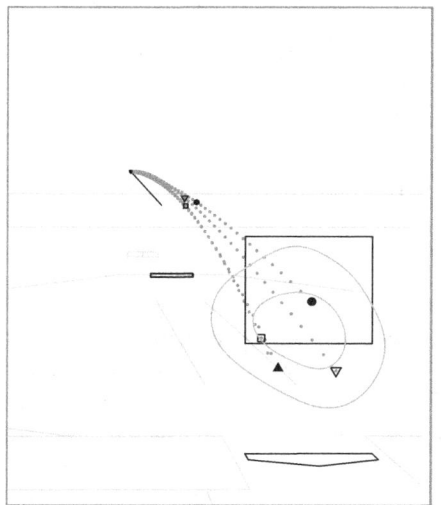

Type		Frequency	Velocity	H Movement	V Movement
●	Fastball	51.4%	91.8 [98]	-3.4 [115]	-16.1 [99]
□	Sinker	18.0%	89.4 [85]	-12.1 [104]	-24.7 [86]
+	Cutter				
▲	Changeup	15.4%	83.9 [94]	-11.9 [97]	-27.4 [100]
×	Splitter				
▽	Slider	15.0%	82.1 [89]	6.6 [108]	-36 [91]
◇	Curveball	0.2%	75.9 [90]	9.6 [107]	-46.8 [103]
⊕	Slow Curveball				
✳	Knuckleball				
▼	Screwball				

Lonnie Chisenhall RF
Born: 10/04/88   Age: 30   Bats: L   Throws: R
Height: 6'2"   Weight: 190   Origin: Round 1, 2008 Draft (#29 overall)

YEAR	TEAM	LVL	AGE	PA	R	2B	3B	HR	RBI	BB	K	SB	CS	AVG/OBP/SLG
2016	CLE	MLB	27	418	43	25	5	8	57	23	70	6	0	.286/.328/.439
2017	CLE	MLB	28	270	34	17	1	12	53	25	55	2	2	.288/.360/.521
2018	CLE	MLB	29	95	11	6	1	1	9	8	12	1	0	.321/.394/.452
2019	PIT	MLB	30	307	35	17	2	9	37	24	60	3	1	.275/.338/.449

Breakout: 1%   Improve: 47%   Collapse: 20%   Attrition: 15%   MLB: 92%
Comparables: David Peralta, Roger Bernadina, Nate Schierholtz

For years, it seemed, Cleveland was waiting for Chisenhall to put it all together. For random spurts, he'd display the offensive skills to make you confident he could hold down an everyday job, only for everything to crater. Every year was the year Chisenhall was supposed to break out, but it never happened. He was a fine glove at the hot corner whose bat was sure to come around, until he wasn't fine there anymore. Then he was a corner outfielder, briefly (and failingly) a center fielder and then back to the corners again. Chisenhall was Cleveland's ultimate enigma, and you thought you'd go gray in the beard waiting for him to become the player many projected when he sat alongside Jason Kipnis atop the pecking order of Indians' prospects. He's been limited to just 365 plate appearances the last two seasons because of calf injuries that cut his season in half in 2017 and lingered throughout 2018. However, on the rare occasion he was healthy enough to swing the bat, he was better than ever before. Now on the wrong side of 30, Chisenhall's small-sample-size success the last two seasons still provides enough promise for him to continue receiving opportunities, but the question becomes whether the calf issues will prevent him from becoming the horse many thought he was meant to be.

YEAR	TEAM	LVL	AGE	PA	DRC+	VORP	BABIP	BRR	FRAA	WARP
2016	CLE	MLB	27	418	94	7.5	.328	-0.3	RF(118): 1.2, 1B(3): 0.0	0.7
2017	CLE	MLB	28	270	110	12.6	.326	-1.5	RF(45): -1.6, CF(19): -0.2	0.8
2018	CLE	MLB	29	95	108	5.1	.366	-0.2	RF(28): 2.1	0.5
2019	PIT	MLB	30	307	106	11.8	.313	-0.1	RF -1, LF 0	1.2

Will Craig 1B

Born: 11/16/94 Age: 24 Bats: R Throws: R
Height: 6'3" Weight: 212 Origin: Round 1, 2016 Draft (#22 overall)

YEAR	TEAM	LVL	AGE	PA	R	2B	3B	HR	RBI	BB	K	SB	CS	AVG/OBP/SLG
2016	WEV	A-	21	274	28	12	0	2	23	41	37	2	0	.280/.412/.362
2017	BRD	A+	22	542	59	26	1	6	61	62	106	1	3	.271/.373/.371
2018	ALT	AA	23	549	73	30	3	20	102	42	128	6	3	.248/.321/.448
2019	PIT	MLB	24	251	25	9	1	9	29	17	67	1	0	.193/.266/.350

Breakout: 2%   Improve: 14%   Collapse: 0%   Attrition: 14%   MLB: 19%
Comparables: Mark Canha, Brock Peterson, Lars Anderson

Entering last year, the knock on Craig was a glove limiting him to first base and not enough power to start there in the majors. The good news is Craig added the thump he was lacking, easily besting his professional highs in home runs and extra-base hits. The bad news is this improvement led to much more of an all-or-nothing approach, featuring a higher strikeout rate and an extreme fly-ball profile that isn't a template for long term success. His infield fly rate of 28 percent exposes a severe uppercut swing that worked in the minors but will be toyed with by major-league pitching. Craig should eventually make it to the majors but, barring a change in approach, he's likely to pad his minor-league home run totals more than he'd want.

YEAR	TEAM	LVL	AGE	PA	DRC+	VORP	BABIP	BRR	FRAA	WARP
2016	WEV	A-	21	274	156	18.3	.322	-2.7	3B(46): 0.1	1.3
2017	BRD	A+	22	542	138	10.8	.335	-7.8	1B(93): 9.4	1.6
2018	ALT	AA	23	549	109	28.6	.288	0.6	1B(122): 8.8	1.3
2019	PIT	MLB	24	251	70	-4.9	.234	-0.4	1B 4	-0.1

Oneil Cruz SS

Born: 10/04/98   Age: 20   Bats: L   Throws: R
Height: 6'6"   Weight: 175   Origin: International Free Agent, 2015

YEAR	TEAM	LVL	AGE	PA	R	2B	3B	HR	RBI	BB	K	SB	CS	AVG/OBP/SLG
2016	DDO	RK	17	211	28	18	5	0	23	22	44	11	5	.294/.367/.444
2017	GRL	A	18	375	51	9	1	8	36	28	110	8	7	.240/.293/.342
2017	WVA	A	18	63	9	2	1	2	8	8	22	0	0	.218/.317/.400
2018	WVA	A	19	443	66	25	7	14	59	34	100	11	5	.286/.343/.488
2019	PIT	MLB	20	251	20	8	1	7	26	8	81	1	1	.179/.203/.308

Breakout: 10%   Improve: 11%   Collapse: 0%   Attrition: 4%   MLB: 11%
Comparables: Alen Hanson, Andrew Velazquez, Gleyber Torres

When scouts talk about a prospect towering over his opponents, it's usually a figure of speech complimenting how much better he is than the competition. Listed at 6'6" but actually closer to 6'8", Cruz literally stands out as a giant among men. Acquired from the Dodgers as part of a package for Tony Watson in 2017, Cruz elevated his prospect status last year with a strong campaign in the Sally League as a teenager facing older competition. Cruz will eventually move off short once he fills out, but it's unclear which corner he'll eventually call home. The larger question revolved around his ability to handle advanced pitching, and whether his large strike zone and gangly frame will be exposed as he moves up the ladder.

YEAR	TEAM	LVL	AGE	PA	DRC+	VORP	BABIP	BRR	FRAA	WARP
2016	DDO	RK	17	211	146	14.8	.382	0.0	3B(32): 4.5, SS(13): -0.7	1.7
2017	GRL	A	18	375	83	13.5	.323	3.2	3B(47): -9.3, SS(30): 0.2	-0.6
2017	WVA	A	18	63	79	3.5	.323	1.0	3B(15): 0.6, SS(1): 0.0	0.1
2018	WVA	A	19	443	129	37.7	.346	2.5	SS(102): -5.9	2.1
2019	PIT	MLB	20	251	31	-11.2	.232	-0.2	SS -1	-1.3

Ke'Bryan Hayes 3B
Born: 01/28/97   Age: 22   Bats: R   Throws: R
Height: 6'1"   Weight: 210   Origin: Round 1, 2015 Draft (#32 overall)

YEAR	TEAM	LVL	AGE	PA	R	2B	3B	HR	RBI	BB	K	SB	CS	AVG/OBP/SLG
2016	WVA	A	19	276	27	12	1	6	37	16	51	6	5	.263/.319/.393
2017	BRD	A+	20	482	66	16	7	2	43	41	76	27	5	.278/.345/.363
2018	ALT	AA	21	508	64	31	7	7	47	57	84	12	5	.293/.375/.444
2019	PIT	MLB	22	251	28	10	2	6	23	15	56	4	1	.219/.267/.354

Breakout: 25%   Improve: 37%   Collapse: 1%   Attrition: 30%   MLB: 39%
Comparables: Taylor Green, Matt Dominguez, Cheslor Cuthbert

Hayes' numbers won't ever leap off the page, but the 21-year-old phenom continued to impress in his climb up the Pirates' organizational ladder. This year, Hayes passed the Double-A test with flying colors, not only holding his own as one of the youngest regulars in the circuit but posting numbers better than many of the older players in the Eastern League. Hayes already projects as a future major league third baseman; the question is if he will provide enough power to be a valuable contributor with the bat. The instincts and glovework continue to improve, and Hayes already looks like he has a higher ceiling than his ex-major-league dad Charlie ever did.

YEAR	TEAM	LVL	AGE	PA	DRC+	VORP	BABIP	BRR	FRAA	WARP
2016	WVA	A	19	276	95	12.4	.304	-1.5	3B(64): 2.0	0.3
2017	BRD	A+	20	482	121	18.0	.331	0.8	3B(108): 20.7	3.8
2018	ALT	AA	21	508	129	38.7	.344	-0.8	3B(116): 9.0	3.5
2019	PIT	MLB	22	251	66	-4.0	.257	0.3	3B 4	0.0

Pittsburgh Pirates 2019

Jung-ho Kang 3B

Born: 04/05/87   Age: 32   Bats: R   Throws: R
Height: 6'0"   Weight: 210   Origin: International Free Agent, 2015

YEAR	TEAM	LVL	AGE	PA	R	2B	3B	HR	RBI	BB	K	SB	CS	AVG/OBP/SLG
2016	IND	AAA	29	57	5	0	0	2	7	7	11	0	1	.146/.246/.271
2016	PIT	MLB	29	370	45	19	0	21	62	36	79	3	1	.255/.354/.513
2018	BRD	A+	31	32	5	2	0	3	11	6	3	1	0	.417/.531/.875
2018	IND	AAA	31	39	4	1	0	0	5	3	5	0	1	.235/.308/.265
2018	PIT	MLB	31	6	0	0	0	0	0	0	1	0	0	.333/.333/.333
2019	PIT	MLB	32	333	43	14	1	12	37	28	73	3	2	.233/.312/.409

Breakout: 1%   Improve: 27%   Collapse: 23%   Attrition: 9%   MLB: 96%
Comparables: Troy Tulowitzki, Carlos Guillen, Vern Stephens

Kang's legal troubles may have ended when he was granted a work visa by the United States in April, but 2018 was yet another lost season for the Korean third baseman. Kang fared terribly in the Dominican Winter League, so the Pirates took their sweet time getting him ready for game action once he came back to the States, sending Kang to instructs in late April before gradually easing him into minor-league action in June. Kang tore up High-A ball and then struggled at Triple-A before a wrist injury sidelined him and knocked him out until the last week of the regular season. The Pirates then inexplicably promoted him for three meaningless major-league contests in September. While he could return in 2019 and be the hitter he was in 2015-2016, there's no historical comp for this sort of comeback. The Pirates declined Kang's $5.5 million option, but quickly brought him back on a bonus-laden one-year deal for $3 million, multiple off-the-field transgressions be damned.

YEAR	TEAM	LVL	AGE	PA	DRC+	VORP	BABIP	BRR	FRAA	WARP
2016	IND	AAA	29	57	66	-0.8	.135	-0.2	3B(13): -0.7	-0.2
2016	PIT	MLB	29	370	129	26.9	.273	-3.7	3B(92): 8.5	3.1
2018	BRD	A+	31	32	196	7.2	.368	0.5	SS(4): -0.6, 3B(2): 0.1	0.4
2018	IND	AAA	31	39	80	-2.7	.267	-1.9	3B(5): -0.6, SS(4): 0.2	-0.2
2018	PIT	MLB	31	6	86	-0.4	.400	-0.4	3B(1): 0.0	0.0
2019	PIT	MLB	32	333	95	5.6	.264	-0.6	3B 4, SS 0	1.1

Kevin Kramer 2B

Born: 10/03/93 Age: 25 Bats: L Throws: R
Height: 6'0" Weight: 200 Origin: Round 2, 2015 Draft (#62 overall)

YEAR	TEAM	LVL	AGE	PA	R	2B	3B	HR	RBI	BB	K	SB	CS	AVG/OBP/SLG
2016	BRD	A+	22	513	56	29	2	4	57	48	63	3	9	.277/.352/.378
2017	ALT	AA	23	234	31	17	3	6	27	17	50	7	2	.297/.380/.500
2018	IND	AAA	24	527	73	35	3	15	59	38	127	13	5	.311/.365/.492
2018	PIT	MLB	24	40	5	0	0	0	4	2	20	0	0	.135/.175/.135
2019	PIT	MLB	25	145	19	8	1	5	16	8	39	2	1	.263/.312/.451

Breakout: 8% Improve: 35% Collapse: 8% Attrition: 24% MLB: 53%
Comparables: David Bote, Joey Wendle, Taylor Featherston

After years of being profiled as a gap hitter without home run power, Kramer changed his hand positioning on the bat and started popping balls over the fence at Triple-A, with 10 of his 13 home runs at Indianapolis coming in his final 328 plate appearances. The Pirates rewarded Kramer with a September promotion and a healthy portion of playing time. It could have gone better. Kramer has hit at every level but is going to have to maintain the power he showed in 2018 to carve out a big-league future. Defensively, he is likely limited to second base; he doesn't have enough range for short or enough arm for third. Kramer will get a long look in 2019.

YEAR	TEAM	LVL	AGE	PA	DRC+	VORP	BABIP	BRR	FRAA	WARP
2016	BRD	A+	22	513	119	18.0	.312	0.8	2B(103): 9.7	2.3
2017	ALT	AA	23	234	124	20.5	.362	1.7	2B(48): -1.6	0.8
2018	IND	AAA	24	527	141	42.2	.392	1.7	2B(82): -6.3, 3B(19): 0.9	3.0
2018	PIT	MLB	24	40	56	-3.3	.278	0.5	3B(7): -0.3, 2B(4): -0.6	-0.1
2019	PIT	MLB	25	145	102	5.3	.335	-0.1	2B 0, SS 0	0.5

Jason Martin CF

Born: 09/05/95 Age: 23 Bats: L Throws: R
Height: 5'10" Weight: 185 Origin: Round 8, 2013 Draft (#227 overall)

YEAR	TEAM	LVL	AGE	PA	R	2B	3B	HR	RBI	BB	K	SB	CS	AVG/OBP/SLG
2016	LNC	A+	20	462	74	22	7	23	75	55	108	20	12	.270/.357/.533
2017	BCA	A+	21	198	34	11	2	7	29	20	42	9	5	.287/.354/.494
2017	CCH	AA	21	320	38	24	3	11	37	19	82	7	6	.273/.319/.483
2018	ALT	AA	22	289	49	13	5	9	34	28	61	7	8	.325/.392/.522
2018	IND	AAA	22	234	20	5	3	4	21	17	52	5	4	.211/.270/.319
2019	PIT	MLB	23	32	4	2	0	1	4	2	8	1	0	.233/.281/.400

Breakout: 18% Improve: 44% Collapse: 5% Attrition: 33% MLB: 58%
Comparables: Brett Phillips, Michael Choice, Lewis Brinson

If he hadn't been included as part of the Astros' four-player package for Gerrit Cole last winter, Martin would be another face in the crowd, a solid but unspectacular outfielder in Houston's seemingly never-ending plethora of prospects. Instead, Martin's interesting, albeit non-elite, mix of skills makes him someone to watch in Pittsburgh as a potential future starter. He picked up at Double-A Altoona where he left off in the Astros organization, showing decent plate discipline, generating power in a park that eats lefties alive and running enough to keep pitchers honest. Martin had a worse time in Indianapolis than Ron Swanson when he found a shuttered Charles Mulligan's Steakhouse, but he gets a pass given it was his first poor performance as a professional at any level.

YEAR	TEAM	LVL	AGE	PA	DRC+	VORP	BABIP	BRR	FRAA	WARP
2016	LNC	A+	20	462	104	27.8	.310	1.2	CF(54): -8.7, LF(26): -5.8	-1.6
2017	BCA	A+	21	198	140	13.7	.333	-1.6	LF(25): 1.1, CF(12): -2.2	0.6
2017	CCH	AA	21	320	118	14.1	.343	1.1	LF(57): -6.9	-0.1
2018	ALT	AA	22	289	140	31.7	.396	-0.7	CF(62): -2.4, LF(6): -0.6	1.4
2018	IND	AAA	22	234	67	-5.5	.261	-0.6	CF(53): -6.5, LF(6): -0.3	-1.2
2019	PIT	MLB	23	32	71	-0.2	.301	0.0	RF -1	-0.1

Calvin Mitchell RF

Born: 03/08/99   Age: 20   Bats: L   Throws: L
Height: 6'0"   Weight: 209   Origin: Round 2, 2017 Draft (#50 overall)

YEAR	TEAM	LVL	AGE	PA	R	2B	3B	HR	RBI	BB	K	SB	CS	AVG/OBP/SLG
2017	PIR	RK	18	185	17	11	0	2	20	24	35	2	3	.245/.351/.352
2018	WVA	A	19	495	55	29	3	10	65	41	109	4	5	.280/.344/.427
2019	PIT	MLB	20	251	18	8	0	6	24	11	76	0	0	.169/.203/.280

Breakout: 5%   Improve: 6%   Collapse: 0%   Attrition: 4%   MLB: 6%
Comparables: Franmil Reyes, Caleb Gindl, Chris Parmelee

In 2018, the Pirates decided to be aggressive with the 2017 second-round pick and start him in full-season ball. For two months, Mitchell was one best hitters in the circuit, then slowly faded as the season wore on—par for the course the first time a prep bat faces a full season of pro ball. Mitchell doesn't possess a sweet swing that generates ooohs and aaahs at the ol' ballyard, but he has a sound approach and knows how to hit, both unusual and coveted traits in a teenager.

YEAR	TEAM	LVL	AGE	PA	DRC+	VORP	BABIP	BRR	FRAA	WARP
2017	PIR	RK	18	185	123	4.4	.303	-0.9	LF(35): 2.6, CF(3): 0.5	0.3
2018	WVA	A	19	495	126	20.4	.347	-4.4	RF(100): 0.5, LF(11): -1.6	0.8
2019	PIT	MLB	20	251	28	-15.5	.215	-0.6	RF 1, LF 0	-1.6

Pittsburgh Pirates 2019

Bryan Reynolds OF
Born: 01/27/95   Age: 24   Bats: B   Throws: R
Height: 6'3"   Weight: 205   Origin: Round 2, 2016 Draft (#59 overall)

YEAR	TEAM	LVL	AGE	PA	R	2B	3B	HR	RBI	BB	K	SB	CS	AVG/OBP/SLG
2016	SLO	A-	21	171	28	12	1	5	30	11	41	2	0	.312/.368/.500
2016	AUG	A	21	66	11	5	0	1	8	3	20	1	0	.317/.348/.444
2017	SJO	A+	22	541	72	26	9	10	63	37	106	5	3	.312/.364/.462
2018	ALT	AA	23	383	56	18	3	7	46	43	73	4	4	.302/.381/.438
2019	PIT	MLB	24	37	4	1	0	1	3	2	10	0	0	.206/.250/.324

Breakout: 10%   Improve: 17%   Collapse: 1%   Attrition: 21%   MLB: 31%
Comparables: Bryan Petersen, Jake Cave, Shane Peterson

When the Pirates finally said their sad, perhaps inevitable goodbye to franchise icon Andrew McCutchen, many fans were underwhelmed by the return for the heart and soul of their team. From a fan perspective, it was difficult to fall in love with a trade that didn't have a true centerpiece, a potential gamechanger who might someday become the next Cutch. It is unfair to compare Reynolds to Cutch, but since he has a higher ceiling than Kyle Crick and you can't scout international slot money without a finance degree, those comparisons will be inevitable. Reynolds is the kind of prospect who underwhelms scouts but has done nothing but perform since being drafted by the Giants in 2016. He falls into that tired "tweener" profile (not good enough defensively for center field, not good enough with the bat for a corner slot), but if he keeps hitting, Reynolds will be in the Pirates' outfield plans sometime in late 2019 or early 2020.

YEAR	TEAM	LVL	AGE	PA	DRC+	VORP	BABIP	BRR	FRAA	WARP
2016	SLO	A-	21	171	123	11.7	.391	1.3	CF(33): -4.1	-0.1
2016	AUG	A	21	66	113	5.5	.452	0.2	CF(11): 1.5	0.3
2017	SJO	A+	22	541	142	35.8	.376	-0.9	CF(50): -4.3, RF(42): -2.9	1.4
2018	ALT	AA	23	383	133	33.4	.362	-0.2	CF(43): -3.2, LF(42): -3.6	1.3
2019	PIT	MLB	24	37	74	0.0	.297	0.0	LF 0	-0.1

Lolo Sanchez OF

Born: 04/23/99   Age: 20   Bats: R   Throws: R
Height: 5'11"   Weight: 168   Origin: International Free Agent, 2015

YEAR	TEAM	LVL	AGE	PA	R	2B	3B	HR	RBI	BB	K	SB	CS	AVG/OBP/SLG
2016	DPI	RK	17	190	19	4	1	0	10	24	18	4	8	.235/.359/.275
2017	PIR	RK	18	234	42	11	2	4	20	21	19	14	7	.284/.359/.417
2018	WVA	A	19	441	57	18	1	4	34	41	72	30	13	.243/.322/.328
2019	*PIT*	*MLB*	*20*	*251*	*24*	*4*	*0*	*5*	*16*	*9*	*56*	*6*	*3*	*.142/.175/.221*

Breakout: 4%   Improve: 4%   Collapse: 0%   Attrition: 2%   MLB: 4%
Comparables: Cedric Hunter, Carlos Tocci, Billy McKinney

Signed as a 16-year-old for a $450,000 bonus out of the Dominican Republic in 2015, Sanchez has impressed scouts with his overall athleticism but lacks any particular tool that stands out. He is a plus runner and advanced defender, but like many of the Pirates prospects profiled on these pages, might never develop the power most hitters need to be an acceptable option in today's game. Sanchez stumbled last year in his first taste of full-season ball, but was only 19 and will get many more opportunities to refine his game against more advanced competition. Sanchez could still grow into his frame but, even if he doesn't, his speed and defense give him a floor as a reliable future backup with the ability to play all three positions in the outfield.

YEAR	TEAM	LVL	AGE	PA	DRC+	VORP	BABIP	BRR	FRAA	WARP
2016	DPI	RK	17	190	112	5.7	.265	0.0	CF(42): 3.2	0.8
2017	PIR	RK	18	234	126	14.5	.295	-0.9	CF(49): 7.6	1.1
2018	WVA	A	19	441	97	14.2	.287	2.7	CF(88): 8.4, LF(19): -2.1	1.3
2019	*PIT*	*MLB*	*20*	*251*	*2*	*-20.0*	*.159*	*0.4*	*CF 3, LF 0*	*-1.8*

Travis Swaggerty CF

Born: 08/19/97   Age: 21   Bats: L   Throws: L
Height: 5'11"   Weight: 180   Origin: Round 1, 2018 Draft (#10 overall)

YEAR	TEAM	LVL	AGE	PA	R	2B	3B	HR	RBI	BB	K	SB	CS	AVG/OBP/SLG
2018	WEV	A-	20	158	22	9	1	4	15	15	40	9	3	.288/.365/.453
2018	WVA	A	20	71	6	1	1	1	5	7	18	0	0	.129/.225/.226
2019	PIT	MLB	21	251	23	5	0	7	21	11	84	2	1	.143/.181/.258

Breakout: 1%   Improve: 1%   Collapse: 0%   Attrition: 1%   MLB: 1%
Comparables: Abraham Almonte, Xavier Avery, Joe Benson

The 10th overall pick in the 2018 draft, Swaggerty inked a $4.4 million deal days after the draft was completed and reported to West Virginia. He didn't miss a beat in his professional debut, showing off the athleticism, defense and speed that made scouts drool over the University of South Alabama product in the first place—though his hits didn't quite drop when he moved up to the Sally League. The primary question about Swaggerty's long-term projection is how much power he'll ultimately develop. There is a lot of swing and miss in his bat, and some analysts believe an all-fields approach will serve him better than a swing-for-the-fences mentality that will pump up his strikeouts and expose him against more advanced pitching. Swaggerty's defense is potentially elite, so regardless of how the bat rounds out, he's a likely future major-league center fielder.

YEAR	TEAM	LVL	AGE	PA	DRC+	VORP	BABIP	BRR	FRAA	WARP
2018	WEV	A-	20	158	146	12.5	.379	0.9	CF(36): -0.6	0.7
2018	WVA	A	20	71	44	-1.2	.159	-0.6	CF(16): 0.7	-0.3
2019	PIT	MLB	21	251	9	-18.0	.180	-0.1	CF -1	-2.1

Cole Tucker SS

Born: 07/03/96   Age: 22   Bats: B   Throws: R
Height: 6'3"   Weight: 200   Origin: Round 1, 2014 Draft (#24 overall)

YEAR	TEAM	LVL	AGE	PA	R	2B	3B	HR	RBI	BB	K	SB	CS	AVG/OBP/SLG
2016	WVA	A	19	67	9	4	2	1	2	4	9	1	1	.262/.308/.443
2016	BRD	A+	19	304	36	12	1	1	25	29	62	5	6	.238/.312/.301
2017	BRD	A+	20	316	46	15	6	4	32	34	70	36	12	.285/.364/.426
2017	ALT	AA	20	194	25	4	5	2	18	21	31	11	3	.257/.349/.377
2018	ALT	AA	21	589	77	21	7	5	44	55	104	35	12	.259/.333/.356
2019	PIT	MLB	22	32	3	1	0	1	3	2	8	1	0	.207/.258/.345

Breakout: 18%   Improve: 33%   Collapse: 0%   Attrition: 21%   MLB: 36%
Comparables: Tyler Wade, Daniel Robertson, Ivan De Jesus

The stat line wasn't impressive outside of the stolen bases, but Tucker continued to improve his rising prospect stock thanks to a full season of health to go along with all-around improvements in his game. While his home run declined, Tucker displayed more lift in his swing and signs that his raw power will translate more into game action. While no one expects 30+ steals in the majors, 20 is a possibility even if Tucker grows into his 6'3" frame. Questions about whether Tucker will remain at short remain, but even if this is the finished product, he projects as a decent defender on the dirt with good on-base skills. Tucker could arrive on the scene in Pittsburgh in 2019 and will be a mainstay wherever or whenever he plays.

YEAR	TEAM	LVL	AGE	PA	DRC+	VORP	BABIP	BRR	FRAA	WARP
2016	WVA	A	19	67	107	6.5	.294	0.5	SS(15): 2.8	0.6
2016	BRD	A+	19	304	83	3.1	.306	-1.1	SS(61): 12.6	1.3
2017	BRD	A+	20	316	139	29.9	.368	1.5	SS(66): -0.4	2.0
2017	ALT	AA	20	194	98	11.4	.304	1.3	SS(42): 0.9	0.7
2018	ALT	AA	21	589	91	37.5	.310	3.4	SS(131): -0.6	1.3
2019	PIT	MLB	22	32	56	-0.3	.251	0.1	SS 0	0.0

Braxton Ashcraft RHP

Born: 10/05/99 Age: 19 Bats: L Throws: R
Height: 6'5" Weight: 195 Origin: Round 2, 2018 Draft (#51 overall)

YEAR	TEAM	LVL	AGE	W	L	SV	G	GS	IP	H	HR	BB/9	K/9	K	GB%	BABIP
2018	PIR	RK	18	0	1	0	5	5	17^2	16	2	2.5	6.1	12	52%	.259
2019	PIT	MLB	19	1	3	0	7	7	32	39	6	5.1	5.1	18	46%	.317

Comparables: Antonio Senzatela, Tyrell Jenkins, Sal Romano

The Pirates' second-round pick in the 2018 draft, Ashcraft was lured away from a commitment to Baylor University with a $1.825 million, over-slot bonus. The 18-year-old hurler throws a 92-mph fastball that can scrape 95, and the sinking action on the heater combined with Ashcraft's imposing frame gave Texas prep school hitters fits. His other pitches need refinement, but that's to be expected from a teenager who has plenty of room to grow, both in physicality and consistency. Ashcraft's five starts in rookie ball were unremarkable, but the Pirates are understandably taking the long view.

YEAR	TEAM	LVL	AGE	WHIP	ERA	DRA	WARP	MPH	FB%	WHF	CSP
2018	PIR	RK	18	1.19	4.58	4.42	0.3				
2019	PIT	MLB	19	1.77	6.55	7.52	-0.8				

Luis Escobar   RHP

Born: 05/30/96   Age: 23   Bats: R   Throws: R
Height: 6'2"   Weight: 210   Origin: International Free Agent, 2013

YEAR	TEAM	LVL	AGE	W	L	SV	G	GS	IP	H	HR	BB/9	K/9	K	GB%	BABIP
2016	WEV	A-	20	6	5	0	15	12	67^2	50	4	3.7	8.1	61	43%	.254
2017	WVA	A	21	10	7	0	26	25	131^2	97	9	4.1	11.5	168	44%	.282
2018	BRD	A+	22	7	6	0	17	16	92^2	76	9	3.7	8.3	85	48%	.272
2018	ALT	AA	22	4	0	0	7	7	35^2	30	4	5.3	6.3	25	43%	.248
2019	*PIT*	*MLB*	*23*	*1*	*1*	*0*	*21*	*0*	*21^2*	*19*	*3*	*5.1*	*8.3*	*20*	*39%*	*.288*

Breakout: 6%   Improve: 14%   Collapse: 9%   Attrition: 19%   MLB: 30%
Comparables: Aaron Blair, Jon Gray, Lucas Sims

In a system that isn't pitching rich, Escobar is arguably Pittsburgh's best pitching prospect this side of Mitch Keller. Escobar throws in the mid-90s with ease and possesses a curve that could become a plus pitch as well. The issues that plagued Escobar in 2017—lack of command and the need for a consistent third pitch—dogged him in 2018 as well. Escobar struggled in his first taste of the upper minors before being suspended by the organization at the end of the year for "violating club policies." How much Escobar can develop his command and improve the change will determine if his future is as a mid-tier starting pitcher or in the bullpen.

YEAR	TEAM	LVL	AGE	WHIP	ERA	DRA	WARP	MPH	FB%	WHF	CSP
2016	WEV	A-	20	1.15	2.93	2.87	1.8				
2017	WVA	A	21	1.19	3.83	2.93	3.6				
2018	BRD	A+	22	1.23	3.98	3.93	1.5				
2018	ALT	AA	22	1.43	4.54	4.05	0.5				
2019	*PIT*	*MLB*	*23*	*1.46*	*5.10*	*5.18*	*-0.1*				

Steven Jennings RHP

Born: 11/13/98 Age: 20 Bats: R Throws: R
Height: 6'2" Weight: 175 Origin: Round 2, 2017 Draft (#42 overall)

YEAR	TEAM	LVL	AGE	W	L	SV	G	GS	IP	H	HR	BB/9	K/9	K	GB%	BABIP
2017	PIR	RK	18	0	2	0	10	10	26^1	31	2	3.4	4.4	13	57%	.305
2018	BRI	RK	19	3	4	0	13	13	65^1	68	5	3.7	7.3	53	46%	.307
2019	PIT	MLB	20	2	5	0	11	11	47^2	58	9	5.9	4.8	25	46%	.318

Comparables: Jordan Hicks, Sandy Alcantara, Clay Holmes

Jennings threw for 2,131 yards and rushed for another 908 as a junior quarterback before being selected in the second round of the 2017 draft. But this was in high school, not college, and the draft in question was for baseball, not football. That's right, Jennings is one of those athletic, projectable types who hasn't done anything noteworthy as a professional to date. Scouts project a mid-rotation ceiling for Jennings, thanks to a good feel for two breaking pitches and a fastball that hit 96 on the gun even though he was wearing a knee brace because of a torn ACL suffered on the gridiron. The raw numbers across two short seasons look rough, but a $1.9 million bonus and a high ceiling will give Jennings oodles of chances.

YEAR	TEAM	LVL	AGE	WHIP	ERA	DRA	WARP	MPH	FB%	WHF	CSP
2017	PIR	RK	18	1.56	4.10	6.12	0.0				
2018	BRI	RK	19	1.45	4.82	4.36	1.2				
2019	PIT	MLB	20	1.88	6.64	7.62	-1.3				

Mitch Keller   RHP

Born: 04/04/96   Age: 23   Bats: R   Throws: R
Height: 6'3"   Weight: 195   Origin: Round 2, 2014 Draft (#64 overall)

YEAR	TEAM	LVL	AGE	W	L	SV	G	GS	IP	H	HR	BB/9	K/9	K	GB%	BABIP
2016	WVA	A	20	8	5	0	23	23	124^1	96	4	1.3	9.5	131	48%	.284
2016	BRD	A+	20	1	0	0	1	1	6	5	0	1.5	10.5	7	47%	.333
2017	BRD	A+	21	6	3	0	15	15	77^1	57	5	2.3	7.4	64	55%	.248
2017	ALT	AA	21	2	2	0	6	6	34^2	25	2	2.9	11.7	45	48%	.280
2018	ALT	AA	22	9	2	0	14	14	86	64	7	3.3	8.0	76	55%	.251
2018	IND	AAA	22	3	2	0	10	10	52^1	59	3	3.8	9.8	57	35%	.366
2019	PIT	MLB	23	2	3	0	8	8	40	37	4	2.9	8.2	37	44%	.293

Breakout: 11%   Improve: 15%   Collapse: 14%   Attrition: 30%   MLB: 39%
Comparables: J.R. Graham, Nick Martinez, Corbin Burnes

As teams get more aggressive about saving money and maximizing player control, service time shenanigans are keeping more and more top-tier prospects in the minors even when they're clearly ready. Although he's the best prospect in Pittsburgh's system, this wasn't the case for Keller. His lack of a third pitch—a slow-to-develop change—has been a story for Keller for his entire career, and his improvement on this front has been incrementally slow. On the plus side, this is the only knock on an otherwise strong profile. His durability and consistency combined with a mid-90s fastball and plus curve rate him a future major league starter with a mid-rotation floor. Keller is almost definitely going to be part of the Pirates plans in 2019, and while the scouting reports keep hammering home the concept of a no. 2 or 3 starter, the clean delivery and confidence give him ace potential down the road.

YEAR	TEAM	LVL	AGE	WHIP	ERA	DRA	WARP	MPH	FB%	WHF	CSP
2016	WVA	A	20	0.92	2.46	2.86	3.3				
2016	BRD	A+	20	1.00	0.00	2.80	0.2				
2017	BRD	A+	21	1.00	3.14	5.75	-0.4				
2017	ALT	AA	21	1.04	3.12	3.36	0.8				
2018	ALT	AA	22	1.12	2.72	3.82	1.5				
2018	IND	AAA	22	1.55	4.82	3.71	1.1				
2019	PIT	MLB	23	1.25	3.92	4.26	0.4				

Pittsburgh Pirates 2019

Travis MacGregor   RHP
Born: 10/15/97   Age: 21   Bats: R   Throws: R
Height: 6'3"   Weight: 180   Origin: Round 2, 2016 Draft (#68 overall)

YEAR	TEAM	LVL	AGE	W	L	SV	G	GS	IP	H	HR	BB/9	K/9	K	GB%	BABIP
2016	PIR	RK	18	1	1	0	9	9	31²	29	1	2.8	5.4	19	57%	.286
2017	BRI	RK	19	1	4	0	12	12	41¹	61	3	4.4	7.0	32	48%	.389
2018	WVA	A	20	1	4	0	15	15	63²	58	7	3.0	10.5	74	47%	.307
2019	PIT	MLB	21	3	5	0	14	14	55²	58	8	4.6	7.5	47	45%	.317

Breakout: 1%   Improve: 1%   Collapse: 1%   Attrition: 2%   MLB: 3%
Comparables: Jayson Aquino, Robbie Ray, Zach Phillips

In recent drafts, the Pirates have taken a fair share of projectable, high-ceiling, prep school arms in the hopes of hitting the jackpot on at least one. At 6-foot-3 and with a lean, lanky frame, MacGregor fits this mold. The mechanics are clean and the fastball already has enough cheddar to be considered major-league ready. As is the case with many minor-league arms, the off-speed stuff is what will make or break MacGregor. The good news is both the curve and change showed signs of improvement. The bad news is MacGregor couldn't stay healthy thanks to a nagging shoulder injury that limited him to 70 2/3 innings. If healthy, MacGregor could take a big step forward in 2019, but shoulder problems have a way of lingering and ruining careers.

YEAR	TEAM	LVL	AGE	WHIP	ERA	DRA	WARP	MPH	FB%	WHF	CSP
2016	PIR	RK	18	1.23	3.13	3.99	0.6				
2017	BRI	RK	19	1.96	7.84	5.18	0.4				
2018	WVA	A	20	1.24	3.25	3.69	1.1				
2019	PIT	MLB	21	1.56	5.16	5.92	-0.4				

LINEOUTS

Hitters

HITTER	POS	TEAM	LVL	AGE	PA	R	2B	3B	HR	RBI	BB	K	SB	CS	AVG/OBP/SLG	DRC+	WARP
Jonah Davis	CF	BRI	Rk	20	241	46	15	6	12	34	27	59	6	5	.306/.398/.612	169	0.7
Nick Franklin	2B	BLX	AA	27	71	10	3	0	2	8	11	7	4	1	.288/.394/.441	119	0.5
	2B	MIL	MLB	27	2	0	0	0	0	0	0	0	0	0	.000/.000/.000	80	0.0
Patrick Kivlehan	OF	LOU	AAA	28	47	3	0	0	0	4	2	15	1	0	.167/.255/.167	46	-0.3
	OF	LVG	AAA	28	390	59	29	4	20	67	30	84	4	3	.314/.372/.588	130	2.1
	OF	ARI	MLB	28	14	3	0	2	0	0	0	6	0	0	.231/.286/.538	71	0.0
Jacob Stallings	C	IND	AAA	28	278	37	22	1	3	40	15	51	1	2	.285/.335/.414	117	0.8
	C	PIT	MLB	28	41	2	0	0	0	5	3	9	0	0	.216/.268/.216	74	0.1
Conner Uselton	RF	BRI	Rk	20	175	15	2	1	0	14	12	31	0	2	.225/.280/.250	48	-1.3

The son of musicians, **Jonah Davis** is accustomed to performing on a big stage; at the age of nine he sang in an opera penned by his father. He has exceeded expectations ever since he was "graded" as a future Division III player at a baseball camp in high school and continued the trend with an impressive Rookie Ball campaign. ⚾ Once a highly regarded prospect, now a utility-playing phoenix, **Nick Franklin** rebrands more frequently than a reality TV star. *Real Catchers of Biloxi* was the 2018 episode. ⚾ **Patrick Kivlehan** played for three organizations in 2018 and got just a handful of MLB plate appearances as a depth piece for the Diamondbacks down the stretch. That appears to be the type of role he's destined to keep. ⚾ At 29.4 seconds per pitch, **Daniel Nava** was the slowest hitter in baseball in 2017. You can't prove that Nava's absence from the majors in 2018 was the reason the median time of games was five minutes faster than they were in 2017, but then again you can't disprove it either. ⚾ A capable backstop, **Jacob Stallings** could be a backup for more than a few teams but was stuck behind two talented catchers in Pittsburgh. He's 29 years old, so he's already in a position where he's going to be Stallings for Time. ⚾ Subpar stats in short-season ball are no kiss of death, but **Conner Uselton** spent most of his year in the circuit as a 20-year-old and has already lost an entire season to a hamstring issue.

Pittsburgh Pirates 2019

Pitchers

PITCHER	TEAM	LVL	AGE	W	L	SV	G	GS	IP	H	HR	BB/9	K/9	K	GB%	WHIP	ERA	DRA	WARP
Dario Agrazal	BRD	A+	23	0	0	0	2	2	8	3	0	0.0	4.5	4	57%	0.38	0.00	4.11	0.1
	ALT	AA	23	5	6	0	15	14	85^2	91	9	1.4	5.5	52	50%	1.21	3.99	4.56	0.8
Jake Barrett	RNO	AAA	26	4	0	8	42	0	53^1	37	3	4.9	11.3	67	48%	1.24	2.87	3.63	0.9
	ARI	MLB	26	0	1	0	7	0	7	8	1	2.6	7.7	6	64%	1.43	5.14	3.94	0.1
J.T. Brubaker	ALT	AA	24	2	2	0	6	6	35	29	1	2.1	9.0	35	63%	1.06	1.80	2.88	1.0
	IND	AAA	24	8	4	0	22	22	119	121	7	2.7	7.3	96	51%	1.32	3.10	4.27	1.7
Nick Burdi	PIT	MLB	25	0	0	0	2	0	1^1	3	1	13.5	13.5	2	33%	3.75	20.25	1.82	0.0
Roberto Gomez	SFN	MLB	28	1	0	0	5	0	9^1	20	0	1.0	7.7	8	51%	2.25	7.71	5.59	-0.1
	SAC	AAA	28	1	3	2	14	0	18	23	3	3.5	6.5	13	42%	1.67	5.00	4.12	0.2
Jesus Liranzo	ALT	AA	23	0	0	4	9	0	12	7	0	2.2	13.5	18	44%	0.83	0.00	1.70	0.5
	IND	AAA	23	2	3	3	32	0	45	31	7	6.2	9.4	47	30%	1.38	5.00	4.33	0.4
Tyler Lyons	SLN	MLB	30	1	0	0	27	0	16^2	24	3	4.3	10.3	19	28%	1.92	8.64	6.32	-0.3
	MEM	AAA	30	1	1	1	7	3	21^2	11	2	2.5	8.7	21	41%	0.78	2.49	3.04	0.6
Alex McRae	PIT	MLB	25	0	1	0	2	0	6^1	8	0	7.1	7.1	5	57%	2.05	5.68	7.80	-0.2
	IND	AAA	25	3	10	1	26	19	117	134	9	3.8	8.0	104	47%	1.57	4.77	4.51	1.3
Dovydas Neverauskas	IND	AAA	25	2	3	4	34	0	46^1	31	2	5.8	11.3	58	52%	1.32	2.53	3.10	1.1
	PIT	MLB	25	0	0	0	25	0	27	30	9	3.3	9.0	27	37%	1.48	8.00	4.83	0.0
Braeden Ogle	WVA	A	20	2	0	0	4	4	17	16	1	5.3	11.1	21	40%	1.53	2.65	3.57	0.3
Aaron Slegers	ROC	AAA	25	5	7	0	15	15	85^1	85	12	2.0	6.0	57	45%	1.22	3.80	5.75	-0.2
	MIN	MLB	25	1	1	0	4	2	13^2	17	3	1.3	4.0	6	39%	1.39	5.27	6.00	-0.1

In an era when every pitcher throws hard and gets strikeouts, **Dario Agrazal** is a pleasant throwback to a simpler world. A control artist who generates contact and allows fans to enjoy batted-ball results, he is going to make baseball better one grumpy, ex-major-league broadcaster at a time. ⓧ Once upon a time, **Jake Barrett** looked like a bullpen fixture, but he did little to convince the Diamondbacks that he truly belongs. With just one minor-league option remaining, Barrett is running out of time to prove he's worthy of a 25-man roster spot. ⓧ **J.T. Brubaker** was a fringy organizational arm until he started touching 97 on the gun in the 2017 Arizona Fall League. If he can keep getting hitters to pound the ball into the ground, Brubaker has a future as a back-end starter or in middle relief. ⓧ Tagged with the "future closer label" ever since he was drafted in 2014, **Nick Burdi** was taken by the Phillies last winter in the Rule 5 draft, traded to the Pirates immediately and spent most of 2018 on the DL recovering from Tommy John surgery, making it next to impossible to watch the Burdi. ⓧ **Roberto Gomez** is tall and chucks a healthy heater, but neither of his breaking balls is up to snuff. ⓧ Four years after Tommy John surgery,

Johnny Hellweg still hasn't been able to find the plate or any semblance of control, for that matter. The Pirates released Hellweg in June so he could sign a contract with the Hiroshima Carp. ⚾ The Pirates nabbed **Jesus Liranzo** off waivers from the Orioles in April. He excites scouts because of a heavy fastball that can hit the upper 90s but needs a refined secondary pitch and improved command if he wants to do more than repeatedly tour the great cities of the International League. ⚾ You know those guys who are always younger than you think, with more time yet to possibly break out? That used to be **Tyler Lyons**. ⚾ After three and a half years toiling in the minors, **Alex McRae** made his major league debut as an emergency fill-in middle reliever, logging two appearances before unceremoniously being removed from the 40-man roster. ⚾ **Dovdas Neverauskas** hails from Vilnius, Lithuania, which claims both Chicago and Madison as sister cities, making it difficult for Vilnius natives who want to root for Neverauskas but must cheer for the Cubs and Brewers due to the complicated, byzantine rules and regulations of sister cities as established during the Paderborn/Le Mans Convention of 836. ⚾ **Braeden Ogle**'s season was cut short after four starts with shoulder inflammation; the promising Pirates prospect hopes to be fully healthy and ready to pitch in 2019. ⚾ **A.J. Schugel** missed nearly all of 2018 with shoulder pain and struggled in the minors after he came back. This was his second shoulder ailment in three years and could mean the end of the line. ⚾ Built like a power forward, **Aaron Slegers** pitches too much like a point guard, dishing up meatballs so hittable he should get assists on all those home runs allowed. ⚾ There are lost seasons, and then there are Lost series finale seasons. **Nik Turley** followed up his ten-year trek to the majors with a PED suspension, a blown elbow, and a DFA. Hopefully he can re-write his own ending to be a little more satisfying.

Pirates Prospects

The State of the System:
I haven't sketched our org rankings out in any sort of detail yet, but man this feels like the fifteenth-best system in baseball.

The Top Ten:

1. Mitch Keller   RHP   OFP: 70   Likely: 60   ETA: 2019
Born: 04/04/96   Age: 23   Bats: R   Throws: R   Height: 6'3"   Weight: 195
Origin: Round 2, 2014 Draft (#64 overall)

The Report: Mitch Keller didn't really change much in 2018, which makes him a bit boring to write about. He didn't need to get much better, mind you, and his numbers above reflect that. His fastball/curve combo is one of the best in the minors. The heater is easy-mid-90s cheese, touching 98 at times. The pitch has ample run that can jam righties assuming they even get the bat on it at all. The curve is a potential plus-plus nightmare in the low-80s. Keller has plus command of both offerings, although his fastball command wobbled at times in 2018. Still, the two-pitch combo here is so good that he hasn't needed much of a changeup.

Coincidentally, "not much of a changeup" appears on the scouting sheet after many of his outings. When his third pitch does peek its head out, it looks more like a firm two-seamer around 90. Again, it hasn't been an issue so far, but even a below-average cambio lurking in hitters' minds could make the overall profile here play up more. Keller has an ideal starter's frame and no red flags in his delivery. He's been quite durable and had a heavy workload by early-20s pitching prospect standards. He's still one of the best pitching prospects in the game, even if no news isn't quite good news here.

The Risks: Medium. Keller isn't really risky per se. He's had a couple small, non-arm injuries the past two seasons, but logged 142 frames this year in the upper minors. The FB/CU combo is as major-league-ready as it gets, but I do worry a bit about his lack of true dominance this year. We're quibbling, but you expect more shoving from one of the five or so best pitching prospects in the game.

Bret Sayre's Fantasy Take: Keller may not have the upside of fellow high-end pitching prospects Alex Reyes or Forrest Whitley, but the combination of proximity, ceiling and floor make him an easy top-five dynasty league arm among farmhands. If the change takes a step forward, it's not hard to envision him

Pittsburgh Pirates 2019

as a solid SP2 putting up similar numbers to future rotation mate Jameson Taillon—very good but not elite ratios, close to 200 strikeouts and a sprinkling of wins. It's likely we'll see Keller by early summer, and he'll be mixed-league worthy from the jump.

2. Ke'Bryan Hayes 3B
OFP: 60 Likely: 50 ETA: Late 2019
Born: 01/28/97 Age: 22 Bats: R Throws: R Height: 6'1" Weight: 210
Origin: Round 1, 2015 Draft (#32 overall)

The Report: Charlie's kid passed the Double-A test with flying colors in 2018. The projection hasn't radically changed, but he continues to look like a future major-league regular. The hit tool is plus. Hayes has a frighteningly quick bat with the whip all the kids are talking about, and he can smoke plus velocity over the third base bag. The swing plane is still pretty flat, but he will show plus raw in BP, and if he ever figures out how to lift the ball more consistently, there is 20-home-run potential here. He marries a sweet swing with a strong approach at the plate, so even if he only ends up socking 40 doubles, the bat should play at a corner spot.

Hayes also checks all the boxes for a plus defender at third base, showing good footwork, sure hands, and a plus, accurate throwing arm. Hayes is an average runner whose speed plays up due to good baserunning instincts. The ultimate projection will depend on how many of those doubles turn into home runs at full maturity.

The Risks: Low. Hayes has an advanced hit tool and approach and offers a plus glove at third base. He's hit in the upper minors, and there may be additional pop to come.

Bret Sayre's Fantasy Take: Among the top 20 fantasy options at the hot corner in 2018, only two of them had fewer than 20 homers. It's a position that in many ways demands the kind of pop that Hayes is unlikely to develop. However, one of these two third baseman was Yuli Gurriel, who is a pretty good approximation from a roto sense of what Hayes could be. There's definitely a place in mixed leagues for a corner bat who can hover close to .300 with 10-15 homers and strong counting stats, but it's the limited upside that will keep Hayes towards the back of the Top 101.

3. Travis Swaggerty OF
OFP: 60 Likely: 50 ETA: Late 2020
Born: 08/19/97 Age: 21 Bats: L Throws: L Height: 5'11" Weight: 180
Origin: Round 1, 2018 Draft (#10 overall)

The Report: Swaggerty went in the top ten of this year's draft on the overall lack of weaknesses in his game, but there is some tools risk here. On the one hand, you can argue that he's a potential five-tool center fielder. This could be technically correct—the best kind of correct—as all five may grade out as 50 or better, but after a down (by first-round college bat standards) junior year at South Alabama, some warts have appeared in the profile. He has had issues with better fastballs at times, and his load can get a little handsy, lengthening the swing and impacting his bat control. His approach is excellent, but might prove a bit too passive against better pitching. There's plus power potential, but it might play down if the hit tool doesn't play to average. Swaggerty has enough speed to stick in center field for now, but might fit better in a corner in a few years. So we could be looking at a .350 OBP, 15-20 home run right fielder instead. That's still a decent ballplayer, but not necessarily an impact one. The physical profile/projection doesn't line up exactly, but the comp I keep coming back to here is "What if Brandon Nimmo went to college?"

The Risks: Medium. Swaggerty has a broad base of skills, but there are some hit tool questions, some positional questions, and a few levels between him and the majors.

Bret Sayre's Fantasy Take: Swaggerty was on fire to start his final college season and it's been a slow march downhill since then for dynasty leaguers. Yet the outfielder still has plenty of potential—it just hinges on his ability to make contact, which makes him no different than most of the good-but-not-elite toolsy hitting prospects on these lists. If it works, he's a .260-ish hitter with 15-20 homers and 25-30 steals who fares a little better in OBP leagues than standard 5×5 ones. He's in the conversation among the top 50 dynasty prospects in the game, but ultimately I think he falls just short.

4

Oneil Cruz SS OFP: 60   Likely: 50
ETA: 2021. This might take a little while.
Born: 10/04/98   Age: 20   Bats: L   Throws: R   Height: 6'6"   Weight: 175
Origin: International Free Agent, 2015

The Report: We suspect that his measurables are now light, and Cruz is one of the most interesting prospects in baseball. In broad strokes, he has a good version of the standard A-ball projectable shortstop skill set: a classic-looking lefty swing geared for contact, good feel for the bat, a plan at the plate, athleticism, soft hands, strong infield instincts and first step, and a real big arm. He also has the monster raw power you'd associate with a guy built like he's two or three years away from playing tight end on Sundays. The downside is that it's basically impossible not to have substantial swing-and-miss when your arms are so long and your strike zone so big. He's shortened up the swing a lot, and yet it's still never going to be less than long just because he's so big.

One of the most frequent conversations I've had with east coast pro scouts over the past year is where the heck Cruz ends up defensively. The easiest guess is right field, since he has a huge arm and might end up with a hulking corner outfield body. But he's improved a lot defensively over the past year, and played a pretty good shortstop in 2018 after spending most of his first two pro seasons at third base.

Could he actually stick at short? If you assume he "only" ends up being something like 6-foot-7 and 220 pounds, he'd be by far the biggest real shortstop in MLB history, but he might still be light and nimble enough for it to work. There's not necessarily any reason a guy that size couldn't play the position if he was appropriately rangy and reliant, especially in the age of aggressive positioning. Having a plus-plus arm can make up for a lot, too.

I'd also suggest the possibility of another unlikely position: center field. I'm not sure he's actually going to get quite as thick as you might guess, and he's a plus runner with good defensive instincts. Doesn't that sound like a center field profile to you? He's far too defensively gifted right now to slide to first base, so he's likely to be among the biggest regulars in history wherever he lands. It is probably going to look weird.

The Risks: We'll default to high, but they're unique and hard to measure. He could be a star and it could take several different forms, from a big power bat at a corner to a well-rounded player up the middle, and we wouldn't be surprised. There's also a real chance he's going to have big problems with velocity or well-located breaking balls due to length, and if he fills out he might fall too far down the defensive spectrum to support the bat. He's so utterly unusual physically that we may be perceiving a higher risk than there actually is, too.

Bret Sayre's Fantasy Take: There's little question that Cruz is a very different kind of prospect than the rest of the folk here. Tall and full of upside, he carries a larger risk profile and more potential power—in our space, we'll almost always take the trade off of the first for the second. A 30-homer bat is a 30-homer bat no matter where he stands, so long as he stands on a major-league field.

5 Calvin Mitchell OF   OFP: 60   Likely: 50   ETA: 2021
Born: 03/08/99   Age: 20   Bats: L   Throws: L   Height: 6'0"   Weight: 209
Origin: Round 2, 2017 Draft (#50 overall)

The Report: My man can hit. Mitchell was assigned to Low-A out of the spring—an aggressive play for a prep in his first full year who just turned 19 and spent the previous summer in the complex. He came out of the chute scorching hot, and continued to hit well enough even as he faded in his first long summer.

Mitchell has a short, effortless swing and the ball jumps off his bat. He's geared to drive the ball, and is already flashing plus power. Throw in an advanced approach and a knack for shooting the barrel with the pitch, and you've got a guy who projects as a 6 hit/6 power bat with room above that. That's the basis for a heck of a player.

We think he'll stick in an outfield corner unless things go bad with the body. He'll probably end up being at least passable out there, if not particularly impressive. He'll never be any sort of stolen base threat or anything, but if you want to be generous, you can even describe him as "sneaky" athletic.

The Risks: Medium. There are always questions about the "hit first, ask questions later" profile until we see it work against MLB pitching, and we're years away from that here. Any hit tool degradation puts his ability to be an above-average hitter into question. Any athletic or defensive degradation slides him to first base, where the bar is much higher.

Bret Sayre's Fantasy Take: And here's the fun guy in the system. A DRC+ of 113 for a teenager in full-season ball is good way to make an impression, and it may catapult Mitchell onto the back-end of the 101 this offseason. There's not much speed in the profile, but his time in West Virginia looked eerily similar to that of current first baseman Josh Bell—and an outfield version of Bell would be a pretty good outcome here, if you believe his talent has yet to quite shine through. There's a .280-25 future, which sadly might be the most valuable realistic ceiling in the organization.

Cole Tucker   SS   OFP: 55   Likely: 45   ETA: Late 2019
Born: 07/03/96   Age: 22   Bats: B   Throws: R   Height: 6'3"   Weight: 200
Origin: Round 1, 2014 Draft (#24 overall)

The Report: Tucker continued to improve at shortstop in 2018, which is a boon for the profile since his bat has not developed at the same pace. While a bit on the tall side for the 6, he moves well on the dirt with above-average lateral range and shows good hands and actions. There's enough arm for the left side, and his quick transfers take some pressure off his throwing. We aren't talking about big shortstop tools here, but Tucker is a "will stick" guy.

At the plate, he's been fine, but not spectacular across two seasons in the Eastern League. Tucker has an athletic frame, but lacks physicality at the plate. There's not much 'oomph.' His hands are good, and the bat control is fine. The bat speed is only average though, and he has struggled at times to identify and deal with Double-A spin. He's not a bad hitter, and you can still bet on some projection in the frame; the profile just lacks the level of impact you could have squinted and seen this time last year.

The Risks: Low. He's a good athlete and a solid shortstop with Double-A time. The bat may not be inspiring at present, but it's the type of skill set that finds itself in the majors even while racking up frequent flier miles to and from Triple-A.

Bret Sayre's Fantasy Take: A quick gander at the steals and you might think this is going to be a more glowing endorsement than it is. Yet Tucker is another good example of why minor league thievery does not translate equitably to the majors. Expectations should be in the 15-20 range over a full season, and when you add that to a meh batting average and middling power (at best), it's a fantasy profile built for 2011.

7. Jason Martin   OF

OFP: 50   Likely: 40   ETA: 2019
Born: 09/05/95   Age: 23   Bats: L   Throws: R   Height: 5'10"   Weight: 185
Origin: Round 8, 2013 Draft (#227 overall)

The Report: The prospect you forgot was in the Gerrit Cole deal—or maybe that was just me—played well in 2018. Martin had a scorching first half of the year in Altoona, followed with some second half struggles for Indianapolis. The overall performance ended up about in line with his 2017, and really his 2016 as well after applying the standard Lancaster adjustment. He's got a very athletic frame—I described him this year as a compact Leody Taveras—but the tools aren't nearly as loud. Martin is merely an average runner with a below-average arm, who's a better fit in left field than center.

The power projection isn't ideal for a corner. He's swing is geared more towards lifting the ball, but he doesn't have the strength to really project for more than average raw, fringy game power. The hit tool is average as well with the added loft, bringing more swing-and-miss. There is some Double-A success here and the ability to at least stand in three outfield spots, so there is likely to be major-league utility as well.

The Risks: Medium. There are strong tweener signs here, and Martin may not hit enough to even "not hit enough for a corner."

Bret Sayre's Fantasy Take: The rest of this system is basically built for undervalued single-digit mono league batters. Unfortunately for those of us in mixed leagues, it leaves a lot to be desired. If you really squint here, you can see something like Harrison Bader. On the bright side, we probably won't have to wait long to find out if he's worthy of a roster spot.

8. Kevin Kramer   2B

OFP: 50   Likely: 40   ETA: Debuted in 2018
Born: 10/03/93   Age: 25   Bats: L   Throws: R   Height: 6'0"   Weight: 200
Origin: Round 2, 2015 Draft (#62 overall)

The Report: If you want to dream on these back-end top ten bats adding some badly-needed power to the profile… well, Kramer managed to do it. Stories like this get written every spring, but the proof was in the performance as Kramer more than doubled his career minor league home run total this season in Indianapolis. While Kramer says this wasn't specifically a loft thing, his swing does appear to be more leveraged for pull-side power now, and there's been a corresponding trade-off with an increased K-rate.

Kramer has experience at three infield spots, but his average foot speed and fringy arm play best at second. He's flipped spots among the Pittsburgh prospect Kevins this year, but he will need to strike out in less than 50% of his plate appearances to maintain that. This is probably the last year I'll need to write about them, but I thought that last year too.

The Risks: Low. He's a major-league-ready middle infielder with some pop.

Ben Carsley's Fantasy Take: I'm bored and there are still two more guys left on this list with the exact same boringness as Kramer.

9. Bryan Reynolds OF
OFP: 50   Likely: 40   ETA: Late 2019
Born: 01/27/95   Age: 24   Bats: B   Throws: R   Height: 6'3"   Weight: 205
Origin: Round 2, 2016 Draft (#59 overall)

The Report: The Pirates spent much of last offseason trading for corner bats without much power projection; it's a bold strategy, Huntington. Reynolds is fun to watch hit though. He's got a pretty swing from both sides, and despite minimal lower half engagement, he fires and maintains balance well. The BP pop is impressive, flashing above-average raw to all fields, but the game swing is more gap-to-gap. Reynolds marries a good approach with good feel for contact, giving him a potential 55 or 60 hit tool.

The problem is that that's going to have to carry the profile. He's fine in left field, but there won't be much defensive value or game power. If the bat falls short of projection he's more of an up-and-down outfielder unless he finds a way to get more of that raw pop into games. Obviously he wouldn't be the first player to figure that out in the majors, and he has some of the markers we tend to look for among power jump guys, but it's not something we can project until we see it.

The Risks: Low. He's fine. He's hit in Double-A. He's fine.

Bret Sayre's Fantasy Take: It's like we've opened up the kitchen cabinet and a mountain of saltines came flying out. If you were into Billy McKinney, you'll love Reynolds. No, not 2014 McKinney.

10. Kevin Newman SS
OFP: 50   Likely: 40   ETA: Debuted in 2018
Born: 08/04/93   Age: 25   Bats: R   Throws: R   Height: 6'1"   Weight: 180
Origin: Round 1, 2015 Draft (#19 overall)

The Report: The Pirates system could be summarized as "Prospect Fatigue: The List." Newman would top that list; I had my reservations about the profile even back when he was a consensus Top 100 type. He was a plus (or better) hit tool guy without anything else to carry the profile. He didn't hit for power. He was fringy at shortstop. A plus hit tool can take you very far, but it better be a plus hit tool. And as the years went on and the pitching got better, it's looked less like a plus hit tool. Newman hit .300 repeating the International League, but looked overmatched in his late-season major league cameo. He's never been the most physical hitter, and the bat may end up Mark Ellis-ish. Newman still doesn't hit for power. He's still fringy at short, but he's a major leaguer now. So he's got that going for him.

The Risks: Low. He's hit in the upper minors, though not as much as you'd like given the rest of the profile.

Bret Sayre's Fantasy Take: The only thing even mildly interesting about Newman is that his stolen base numbers spiked in 2018—but after nearly reaching 30 in the minors, he was caught on his only attempt in the show. This concludes the test of our emergency broadcast system.

The Next Five:

11 Luis Escobar   RHP
Born: 05/30/96   Age: 23   Bats: R   Throws: R   Height: 6'2"   Weight: 210
Origin: International Free Agent, 2013

Escobar's strikeouts evaporated some against better hitters in 2018, but the building blocks for a durable backend starter remain. The fastball bumps 95 as a starter, although it generally sits in a more average velo band. It's a heavy pitch with some two-seam run at times as well. Escobar has a fairly long arm action and a high-three-quarters slot so he's not always on top of the pitch and it can sit up in the zone, but even then it can be difficult to elevate. He offers a potentially average curve and change as well. The curve can get a little humpy and ride high as well, but it flashes tight 12-5 action. The change shows some fade, but can be too firm. Escobar is confident enough to throw it early in counts and to both sides though. It's a collection of three averageish pitches, a frame built for logging innings, and the same No. 4/5 starter projection here. Escobar has shown upper-90s velocity at times in short bursts, so there is the potential for a fastball/curve reliever here as well.

12 Lolo Sanchez   OF
Born: 04/23/99   Age: 20   Bats: R   Throws: R   Height: 5'11"   Weight: 168
Origin: International Free Agent, 2015

Your typical speed-and-defense center field prospect with a questionable hitting projection. Sanchez is a plus to plus-plus runner with impressive range in the outfield. He was an above-average hitter in Low-A this year, jumping from the GCL while he was still 18. Mitchell is an obvious point of comparison as a similarly-aged outfield mate who we're projecting a lot higher here, and while Sanchez obviously has greater projection everywhere else but the plate than Mitchell, I just don't like the bat path and can't project similar power. If Sanchez can start squaring up and gets more balanced, there's a shot for a regular here with all the secondary skills, but it's a longer shot and this is a deep system as 5/4 types go.

13 Tahnaj Thomas   RHP
Born: 06/16/99   Age: 20   Bats: R   Throws: R   Height: 6'4"   Weight: 190
Origin: International Free Agent, 2015

Thomas appears to be the underlying reason for the Luplow/Gonzalez/prospects swap, at least from Pittsburgh's side. Thomas signed with the Indians as an infielder out of the Bahamas for $200,000 late in his bonus period, but quickly converted to the mound. He's spent two seasons kicking around the complexes, and picked up notoriety in Arizona this year as an athletic arm strength guy with some feel for spin. "Targeting players from emerging baseball markets" and "targeting guys at the beginning of breakouts at the lowest MILB levels" are both trendy plays for aggressive teams, and Thomas fits the bill here. He's still a million miles away from the majors, however: Watch him, while remembering that his future could take nearly any form.

14 Will Craig 1B
Born: 11/16/94 Age: 24 Bats: R Throws: R Height: 6'3" Weight: 212
Origin: Round 1, 2016 Draft (#22 overall)

Craig was a 23-year-old first baseman who hit .248/.321/.448 in Double-A this year. I often like to say that minor-league production, good or bad, exists primarily to be explained. But on rare occasions it is perfectly descriptive in and of itself. The slash line above—with accompanying demographic context—paints a picture in your mind. A hulking slugger with a bit of a stiff swing and commensurate swing-and-miss issues. Plus raw that plays down in games accordingly. I used a "right-handed Rowdy Tellez" comp earlier in the season, and the range of outcomes here is similar. Craig has all the usual pitfalls that we associate with R/R first base types, and there isn't really a role for a right-handed corner dude with that line in 2019. But hey, Rowdy Tellez hit a boatload of doubles last September.

15 Rodolfo Castro 2B
Born: 05/21/99 Age: 20 Bats: B Throws: R Height: 6'0" Weight: 200
Origin: International Free Agent, 2015

And now we have a 19-year-old middle infielder who hit .231/.278/.395 in Low-A this year, and hey, that serves as a serviceable description as well. The shape of the performance gives you the right idea for sure. Castro has a well-developed frame and there is decent raw power here. There's better feel for contact than a .231 batting average in the Sally would suggest, but he tends to swing at far too many pitches out of the zone. That makes him a pesky hitter against A-ball arms, but potentially a windmill against better ones. Castro is a good defender at the keystone, and his arm likely limits him to the right side of the infield. He's a fun enough prospect with a bit to dream on, but likely would be more of a personal cheeseball or low minors sleeper in a deeper system. I should just check the utility infielder box and move on, but sometimes you like a guy more than you should.

Pittsburgh Pirates 2019

Others of note:

Travis MacGregor, RHP, Low-A West Virginia

I had MacGregor on my Sally watchlist when initial rosters came out, and he might've been the buzziest guy coming into the season on a West Virginia roster that turned out to be pretty loaded. I got to see him in their mid-May series in Lakewood, and I spent most of the first two innings of his start perplexed at why his stuff was way down. He exited in the second with an undisclosed arm injury, missed six weeks, came back for a bit, and was shut down again with a forearm problem in August. You can probably already guess that this ended in Tommy John surgery, which Pirates Prospects reported happening in September. Before the injury, he was a tall, projectable righty already sitting in the low-90s from a tough arm angle, with the changeup and curveball flashing as secondaries. We'll see what comes back in 2020.

Braeden Ogle, LHP, Low-A West Virginia

MacGregor's West Virginia rotation mate is also his mirror image in a lot of ways. While not quite as buzzy in Bristol last year, Ogle offers a sneaky-fast low-90s fastball that comes from a tough angle given his low slot and uptempo, crossfire delivery. He can spot the fastball to both sides and it will show good boring action in on righties. He was throwing a slider in April, which had some good short tilt to it; it's a projectable secondary. He has a changeup as well. There's also the shoulder soreness that ended his season in April, which is in some ways even more concerning than actual Tommy John surgery. We'll see what comes back in (hopefully) 2019.

Braxton Ashcraft, RHP, GCL Pirates

Looking above, you might be a bit concerned about the Pirates dearth of pitching prospects. Fair enough. They tried to rectify this in the draft, popping Ashcraft in the second round, and Gunnar Hoglund in the comp round. Hoglund elected to go to Ole Miss, so the Pirates are left betting—like many, many other orgs—on a projectable prep arm from Texas. He added some velocity across the spring—touching the mid-90s—and has the kind of lean, limby frame you can bet on adding some more over the next few years. There's some feel for a breaking ball, although he will slow down and cast it at times. If you like fun facts, he caught 37 touchdowns as a high school senior, so there are gonna be worse athleticism bets out there. We'll see what he shows in 2019.

Top Talents 25 and Under (born 4/1/93 or later):

1. Mitch Keller
2. Ke'Bryan Hayes
3. Travis Swaggerty

4. Keone Kela
5. Oneil Cruz
6. Calvin Mitchell
7. Cole Tucker
8. Jason Martin
9. Kevin Kramer
10. Bryan Reynolds

A comparison between the 2018 and 2019 versions of this list tells you quite a bit about the state of the Pirates. Last year, there were five major-leaguers represented; this year, just one. Josh Bell, Trevor Williams, and Chad Kuhl turned 26 and graduated (along with Joe Musgrove, who hit this milestone a month before his trade from the Astros). These newly minted late-twenty-somethings join an impressive cohort of 27-year-olds—Jameson Taillon, Felipe Vazquez, Gregory Polanco, Nick Kingham, Adam Frazier.

This is good, right? In a vacuum, you want a core of late-twenty somethings, especially given that the two most prominent veterans on the team, Starling Marte and Chris Archer, each just blew out thirty candles in the past few months. With the productive bulk of the roster between 26 and 30, this team should be squarely in its window of contention. The problem, of course, is that the Pirates don't play in a vacuum; they play in the NL Central, where three other teams are loaded to the gills. Given the competition of the Brewers, Cubs, and Cardinals, this is a roster suffering from a relative shortage of both quality and depth.

The lone big-leaguer, former Rangers closer Keone Kela, slots in just after the top three prospects. And, yes, Kela is quite good at what he does, and when his heat-and-hook combo is on, he's well-nigh unhittable. All the same, he's a relief arm. Kela would be the prime candidate to step in for Felipe Vazquez in the case of injury, trade, or banishment from the ninth inning, but it's not like the Pirates don't have other strong bullpen options (Richard Rodriguez, for one) at the ready. Still, Kela is a clear several notches above the only other viable 25-and-under candidate for this list, Michael Feliz, whose first season in Pittsburgh was bogged down by both injury and inconsistency.

One final Yinzer shout-out to Austin Meadows and Tyler Glasnow, who would feature prominently on the front half of this list were they still in the Steel City. They, however, are part of a much more crowded crew of young talent in Tampa Bay, swapped out for Archer in a deadline deal. Certainly, Meadows and Glasnow were prime candidates for changes of scenery, but if Archer doesn't earn that "ace" label quickly, Bucs fans might find their wandering eyes checking out Rays box scores, wondering "what if…"

Part 3: Featured Articles

The Hole in The Shift is Fixing Itself

Russell Carleton

I've been on a bit of a mission against The Shift of late. I'm not out to get The Shift for the usual reasons that people oppose it. The words "the right way to play the game" won't be found on my lips. If a team wants to pursue a strategy that is within the rules and it works, then by all means, they have my blessing (not that they need it). Instead, my concern with The Shift is a worry that it doesn't work, or at least that it has a flaw that needs fixing.

The data show that while The Shift does a decent job of preventing singles on balls in play (what it's supposed to do), it also increases the number of walks that happen in front of it, and the number of additional walks outweighs the number of singles saved. It's a problem because you can't throw a guy out if he gets to walk to first base.

But the "why" was important. It seemed that The Shift was changing the way in which pitchers pitched. We saw that there were fewer fastballs thrown in front of The Shift than we might otherwise expect, and that pitchers tended to stay out of the strike zone a little more. Not by a lot. In fact, it might not even be visible to the naked eye. The percentage of pitches that are out of the zone goes from 51.0 to 53.3 from a standard defense (two right/two left) to a full shift (three on one side). That difference stands up even after we control for the types of hitters that get shifted against. And it's enough to drive up the walk rate to where it cancels out the benefits that teams thought they were getting with The Shift… and then some.

But there was some hope. I found that when individual pitchers stayed closer to the in-zone/out-of-zone mix that they used without The Shift on, they could still get the benefits of The Shift without the walk problems. So, in theory, a team could simply figure out a way to convince its pitchers to not fall prey to the walk trap and The Shift would once again be their friend.

It's reasonable to think that some teams might be more hip to this idea than others. Maybe some figured it out a year before the others. Maybe they were better at getting the message across to their pitchers. Or, maybe no one has figured it out yet.

Warning! Gory Mathematical Details Ahead!

I used data from 2015-2017, made available through MLB's data portal, Baseball Savant. They are kind enough to note when teams are using an infield shift (three fielders on one side of second base), as opposed to a "strategic shift" (someone's playing a bit out of position, but it's not quite that drastic) or a "standard" alignment.

Since we're doing this by team, I can't just look at raw walk rates, because we know that some teams have good pitchers and others have not-so-good pitchers. Some have a mix of both. I used the log-odds ratio method to take into account a batter's general walking proclivities, and a pitcher's as well, and then shoving them into a binary logistic regression. Then, I asked the computer to generate a specific coefficient for each team's pitchers, for when they went into The Shift and how that affected their walk rate.

Using those coefficients, I was able to project what would happen if a league-average pitcher faced a league-average hitter (which we expect would product a league-average walk rate; from 2015-2017, 7.7 percent of plate appearances ended in a walk) and then just switched his hat. Here's the top five and the bottom five:

Top 5 Teams	Projected Shift Walk Rate	Bottom 5 Teams	Projected Shift Walk Rate
Rockies	6.2%	Rangers	11.2%
Pirates	6.7%	Mets	10.4%
Indians	7.2%	Dodgers	10.2%
Astros	7.3%	Cardinals	9.9%
Braves	7.7%	Tigers	9.7%

There are probably people out there right now trying to figure out what the common thread is among the top and bottom teams. I'm sure, because this is Baseball Prospectus, people are already trying to make the case that sabermetric "early adopters" have some sort of edge here. I think that the more interesting piece is that by the time you get to fifth place in The Shift, we're at league average.

As a sanity check, I examined the issue on a pitch-by-pitch level, looking at how often pitchers threw their pitches in the GameDay strike zone, and again using the same basic methodology and getting team-specific coefficients. The names on the list re-arranged themselves, but the idea was the same, and the two lists correlated with an R of .593.

There's a reason that I don't usually do this type of leaderboard post. I don't really know what the Rockies, Pirates, Indians, Astros, and Braves have in common, or what they have that the bottom five don't. I can put a shrug emoji here and say, "Well, it must be something!" but that seems like a cop-out. Instead, I'd like to present another table and suggest that the table above doesn't even really matter anymore.

Year	League Percent Outside K Zone (Full Shift)	League Percent in K Zone (No Shift)	Difference
2015	54.1%	51.1%	3.0%
2016	53.3%	50.9%	2.4%
2017	52.6%	50.9%	1.7%
2018	52.0%	50.7%	1.3%

The hole in The Shift is fixing itself, and it's coming down really fast league wide. In my earlier work on The Shift, I suggested that until teams stopped having such a huge difference between their out-of-zone rate with and without The Shift on, there would just be too many walks for The Shift to make sense. It seems that all 30 of them have been working toward just that. I once estimated that it takes about 10 years for an idea to filter its way through baseball. At this rate, it looks like teams are going to catch up a lot faster than that. And yeah, they're all saber-smart now.

It's likely that whatever magic it was that the Rockies and Pirates had has made its way to Texas and Queens. Or is at least on its way. And if teams are committing to fixing the walk problem, then it's likely that they will continue shifting and shifting a lot.

And eventually it's going to actually make sense for them to do it.

—Russell Carleton is a former author of Baseball Prospectus and now an analyst for the New York Mets.

The State of the Quality Start

Rob Mains

One of the seven things you (probably) didn't know about the 2018 season is that quality starts—defined as a start lasting six or more innings with three or fewer earned runs allowed—as a percentage of total starts cratered to an all-time low of 41 percent. I want to look a little more deeply into this, since it's been a while (May of 2016, to be exact) since I've examined quality starts.

The term *quality start* is credited to *Philadelphia Inquirer* sportswriter John Lowe. It's been derided ever since he coined it in December of 1985. Three runs in six innings? That's a 4.50 ERA! In what world is that a measure of quality?

Let's start with that criticism. It's true that 3 x 9 / 6 = 4.5. (You came here for this sort of high-level math, right?) But it's also true that type of start, meeting the bare minimum for earning a quality start, is unusual. Here's the proportion of quality starts in which the pitcher lasted exactly six innings and yielded exactly three earned runs. (I'm going to confine this analysis to the 30-team era, 1998-present. Almost all data retrieved in this article is via the Baseball-Reference Play Index.)

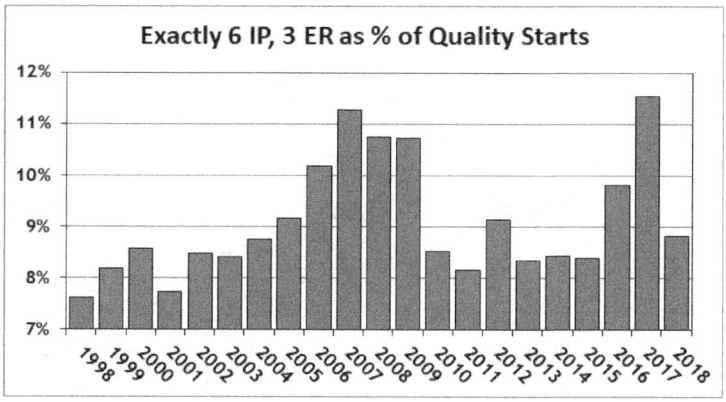

There were 1,997 quality starts in 2018. Only 176, or fewer than one in 11, featured a pitcher going six innings and allowing three earned runs. Put another way, the percentage of quality starts that resulted in a 4.50 ERA (8.8 percent) is

Pittsburgh Pirates 2019

less than half the percentage of games in which a batter hit two home runs and his team lost (22.5 percent; 237-69 won-lost). That doesn't impugn hitting two homers.

So if a 4.50 ERA isn't the norm, what is? How good are quality starts?

Pretty good, it turns out. First, on a team level:

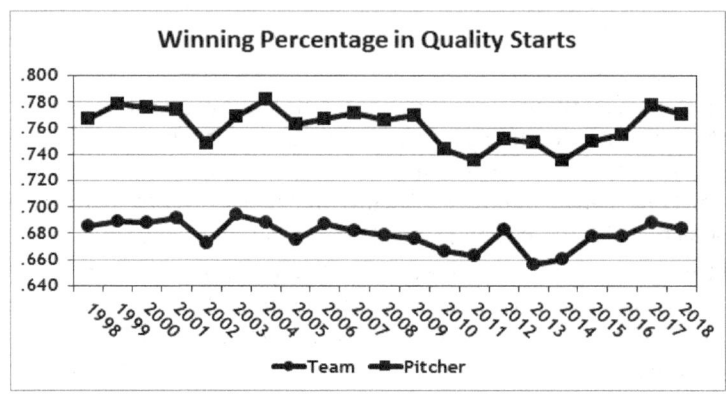

Teams receiving a quality start from their pitcher won 68.4 percent of their games in 2018, in line with the 30-team era average of 67.9 percent. A team with a .684 winning percentage wins 111 games. Getting a quality start is definitely a good thing. Individual pitchers throwing quality starts have a higher winning percentage because a big slice of team losses is assigned to a reliever.

If teams do well in quality starts, how well do the starting pitchers do? Again, very well.

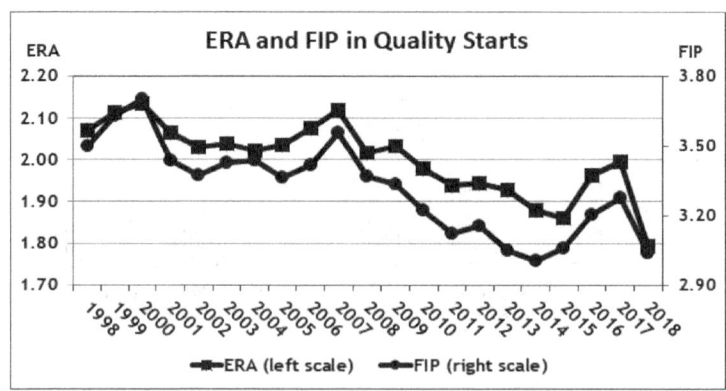

Pitchers in quality starts had a 1.79 ERA (blue line) in 2018, *the lowest in the 30-team era*. Their FIP was higher, 3.04, but still excellent. In the 30-team era, only 2014 had a lower FIP for quality starts, 3.01.

But, of course, the run environment in 2014 was different. Teams in 2014 scored 4.07 runs per game, the fewest in a non-strike year since 1976. They scored 4.45 runs per game in 2018. So surrendering a 3.04 FIP in 2018 is more impressive than 3.01 in 2014. Accordingly, let's look at ERA and FIP in quality starts relative to league averages.

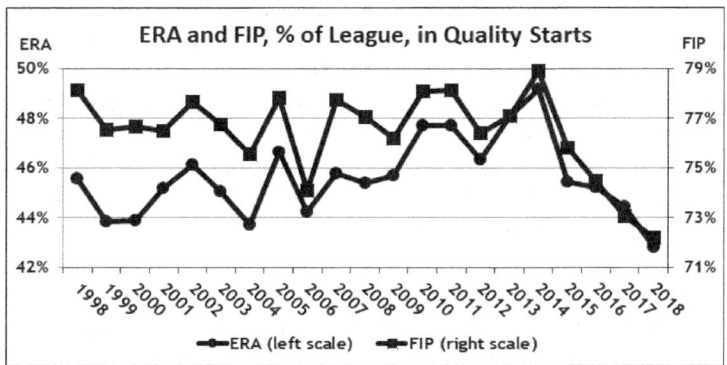

This tells a more dramatic story. Starting pitchers in 2018 gave up a 4.19 ERA and a 4.21 FIP. Starters in quality starts gave up a 1.79 ERA, 43 percent of the league average. Starters in quality starts gave up a 3.04 FIP, 72 percent of the league average. Both of these marks represent lows in the 30-team era.

The takeaway here is this: *Quality starts are better, relative to other starts, than they've ever been over the past 21 years.*

Maybe during the winter I'll look at this over a longer arc of time. For now, though, we can definitively say quality starts are the best they've ever been since the Diamondbacks and Rays joined the majors.

Yet, paradoxically, they're down.

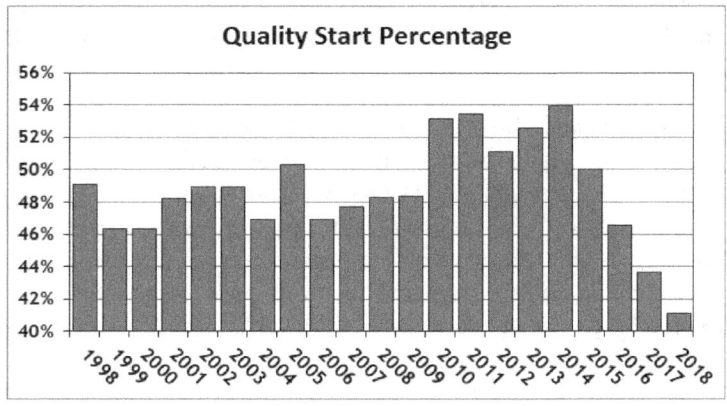

This graph covers only the 30-team era. In my article last week, though, I looked at the years 1908-2018. The result was the same. The 41 percent of starts in 2018 that were quality starts are an all-time low, well below the runners-up: 1930's 43 percent (the year teams scored an all-time record 5.55 runs per game) and last year's 44 percent.

The normal explanation for a dip in quality start percentage is an increase in scoring. When teams score a lot of runs, it's harder for starting pitchers to last six or more innings and limit opponents to three earned runs. From 1998 to 2014, the correlation between runs scored per game and the percentage of starts that were quality starts was -0.94. That means there was an extremely close relationship: More runs, fewer quality starts. Too small a sample? Go back to the start of the Expansion Era, 1961, and the relationship is even more negative, a -0.95 correlation, though 2014.

But that's broken down over the past four years:

- 2015: Runs per game increased from 4.07 to 4.25, quality start percentage decreased from 54.0 to 50.1. Yes, that's a negative relationship, but the regression model would predict a decline of 1.5 percentage points. We got 3.9 instead.
- 2016: Runs per game increased from 4.25 to 4.48, quality start percentage decreased from 50.1 to 46.6. Past experience would suggest a decline of just 1.8 percentage points. We got 3.4.
- 2017: Runs per game increased from 4.48 to 4.65, quality start percentage decreased from 46.6 to 43.6. Again, the direction's right, but the magnitude isn't. Using the relationship from 1998 to 2014, that increase in scoring should've reduced quality starts by 1.3 percentage points, not 2.9.
- 2018: Runs per game declined from 4.65 to 4.45. That should've resulted in the quality start percentage moving in the other direction, rising 1.6 points. It didn't. It fell 2.6 points, as noted, to an all-time low.

Granted, we're talking about just four years here. Maybe they're outliers. But I don't think they are. Quality starts, as noted, are as good or better than ever. But they're rarer than ever as well. And I think I know why.

To get a quality start, you need to allow three or fewer earned and pitch at least six innings. That's 18 outs. Here's a graph showing the number of starting pitchers who limited their opponents to three or fewer earned runs but got pulled after pitching at least five innings but fewer than six:

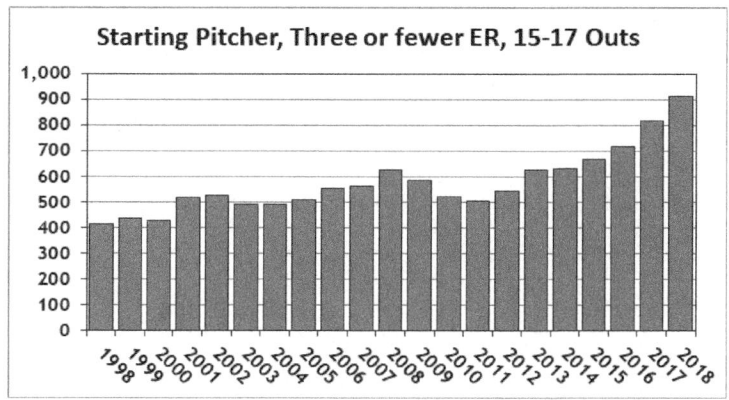

A pitcher getting 15 outs pitched five innings. A pitcher getting 16 outs pitched 5 1/3. A pitcher getting 17 outs pitched 5 2/3. More than ever before, pitchers are being removed from games in which they are within 1-3 outs of a quality start, falling just short of the six-inning finish line. Widespread acknowledgement of the times-through-the-order penalty and a flotilla of available bullpen arms is making the quality start simultaneously both more excellent and more rare.

Which is ironic, given that we saw a new post-war quality start record this season:

Rank	Pitcher	Season	Consecutive QS
1	Jacob deGrom	2018	24
2	Bob Gibson	1968	22
-	Chris Carpenter	2005	22
4	Johan Santana	2004	21
5	Luis Tiant	1968	20
-	Mike Scott	1986	20
-	Jake Arrieta	2015	20
8	Robin Roberts	1952	19
-	Tom Seaver	1973	19
-	Jack Morris	1983	19
-	Greg Maddux	1998	19
-	Josh Johnson	2010	19
-	Jon Lester	2014	19

While there have been longer streaks spread over multiple seasons, no pitcher since World War II threw more consecutive quality starts in one year than Jacob deGrom this year. The fact that he did in a year in which quality starts were the rarest they've ever been adds to the accomplishment.

—Rob Mains is an author of Baseball Prospectus.

Heads-Up Hacking—The First Pitch

Matthew Trueblood

Batters fell behind in a higher percentage of all plate appearances in 2018 than in any previous season for which we have pitch-by-pitch data. That kind of granular information goes back only to 1988, but we might safely assume (given all we know about baseball as it had been before that, and as it has been in the years since) that batters have *never* fallen behind at a higher rate than they did last season.

Through the 1990s, the percentage of all plate appearances that began 0-1 hovered in the high 30s and low 40s. In the 2000s, it rose steadily but slowly, through the mid-40s. In 2018, 49.8 percent of all trips to the plate began 0-1. That, as much as anything, captures in microcosm the nature of hitting in MLB today.

A countdown clock toward strike three begins ticking almost the moment a batter takes his place in the box. The league's adjusted OPS+ on the first pitch was higher in 2018 than ever before, and that has been true in most of the last 10 seasons. Batters hit .264/.289/.442 in all plate appearances in which they swung at the first pitch last season, and .241/.330/.395 in all plate appearances in which they took that first offering.

The percentage differences in batting average and isolated power there favor swinging at the first pitch by more than in any season since 1988, while the difference in on-base percentage favors taking by more than ever. If you want to get on base at a decent clip, it's a good idea to be patient, but you run the risk of missing the only chances you'll get to produce power.

Pittsburgh Pirates 2019

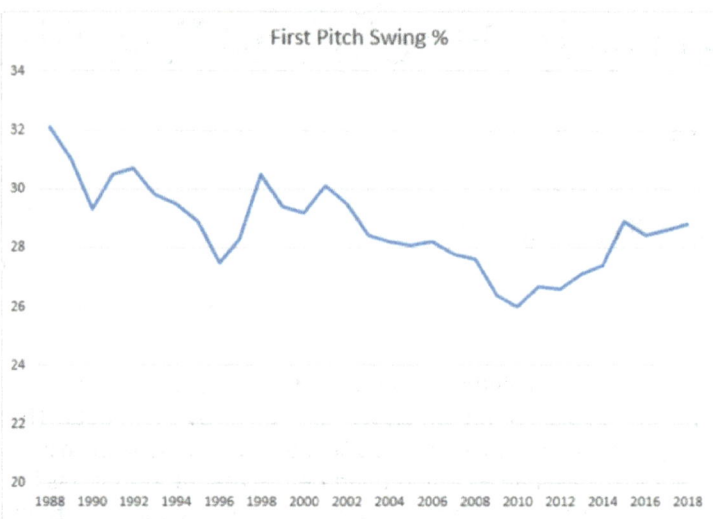

The league swung at the first pitch 28.8 percent of the time in 2018. With the isolated exception of 2015, that's the highest that number has climbed since 2002, but it might not be high enough. With the help of BP research maven Rob McQuown, I looked at the aggregate Called Strike Probability (CSProb) on the first pitch for each season since 2008, when the implementation of PITCHf/x first made measuring that possible. It's risen sharply during that period.

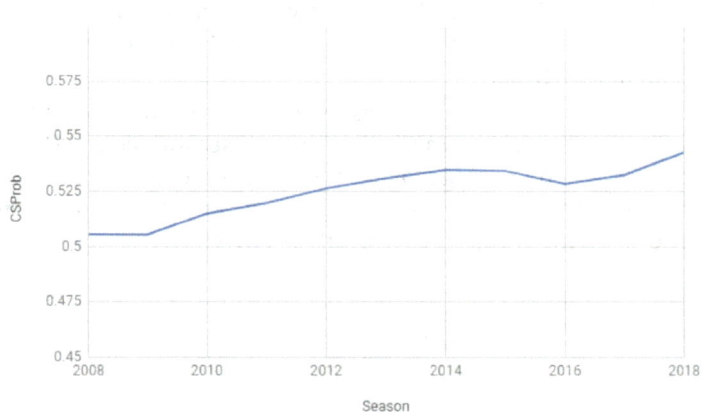

Called Strike Probability, First Pitch of PA (2008-2018)

Called Strike Probability is exactly what it sounds like: a pitch with a given CSProb has roughly that chance of being called a strike, if not swung at. In 2018, a batter who took 100 first pitches from a random sampling of the league's pitchers might expect to fall behind 54 or 55 times—up from 50 or 51 times in 2008. Almost regardless of pitch type (and, notably, especially in the case of fastballs), the first pitch tends to have more of the zone right now than ever before.

Pitchers are better at throwing strikes. They have better stuff, and believe more in their ability to miss bats within the zone. Perhaps most importantly, they know that batters are looking for one thing on the first pitch: a fastball. If they don't get it, they're likely to take the pitch. Check out how the use of sinkers and four-seamers on the first pitch has changed in a decade:

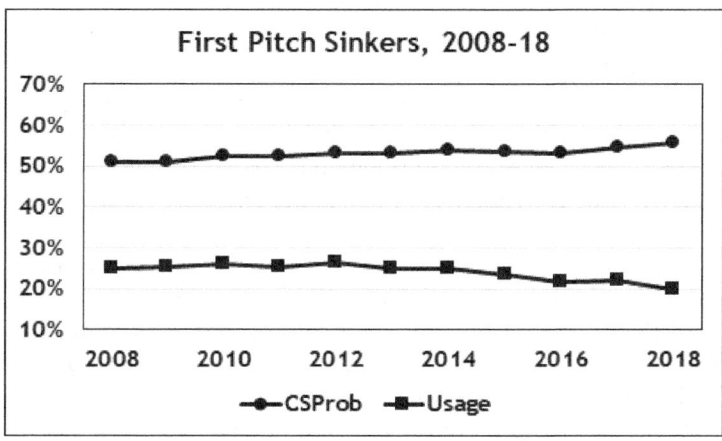

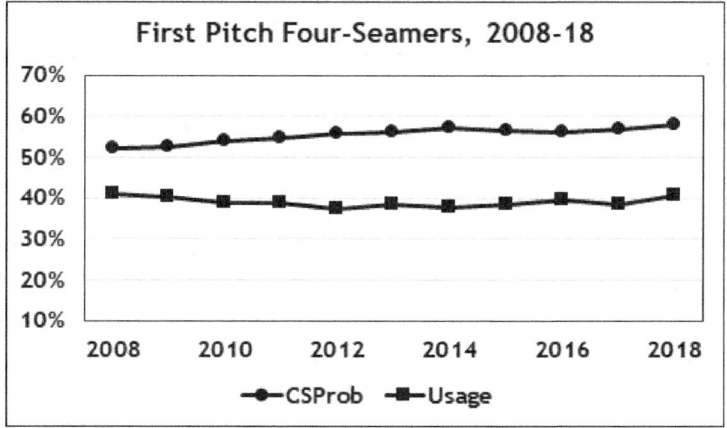

The sinker is losing its place in baseball, but the rate at which pitchers have thrown it on the first pitch hasn't dropped any faster than its usage rate in other counts. Pitchers have actually gone to their four-seamer *more* often to open counts, in the last few years, after a dip in the 2012-2015 period. What's really changed, though, and what shows up in both charts above, is that pitchers are catching more of the zone with first-pitch fastballs than they were a decade ago, or a half-decade ago. They're attacking right away, even with the pitch they know batters are expecting. The message is pretty clear: batters are being too passive.

Sliders, curves, and changeups each have more of the zone when thrown on the first pitch than they did several years ago, too, though the effect is less pronounced. Pitchers have seen the numbers; they know batters are doing better on the first pitch itself. They still feel safe throwing more and better strikes than ever before, figuring they'll come out ahead as long as they keep getting ahead to open each battle.

The Moneyball revolution brought an increased league-wide focus on OBP, which resulted in a de facto mandate to take a more patient tack at the plate. It worked very well for a while, as batters with poor plate discipline were compelled to either adjust or be expelled from the league, and pitchers with poor control were slowly weeded out.

However, concurrent with that revolution, and spurred by it in some ways, was the evolution of the pitching paradigm that now dominates the game. As batters ratcheted up their focus on inflating pitch counts and working walks, pitchers honed theirs on throwing strikes and missing bats. The league's understanding of what makes a good pitcher improved at least as much, from the mid-1990s through the mid-2000s, as its understanding of what makes a good hitter. As amphetamines and other performance-enhancing drugs were phased mostly out of the game, and as PITCHf/x broke onto the scene, individuals and teams learned how to exploit the evolved approaches of even the smartest hitters.

The ability to avoid making outs is still the most valuable one in baseball, but the magnitude of its eclipse of slugging is smaller than ever. To a greater extent than power, on-base skills derive their value from chaining—from the on-base skill levels of the players on either side of a given individual. Eleven years ago, when the housing crisis hit, people learned the hard way that the value of their homes depended a good deal on the values of their neighbors' homes. The same wasn't true, though, of their cars. So it is now, with OBP and SLG.

The global OBP in 2018 was .318. The only seasons since the Dead Ball Era in which the league got on base at a worse clip were 2013-2015, 1988, 1971-1972, and 1963-1968. This is all happening despite the aforementioned evolution of the science of hitting. It's happening despite a shift in approach and focus, one that would steer OBP ever higher, if only it were working.

Instead, it's sitting at a low ebb, and while it does so, even guys who get on base often are a little less helpful than they were 10 years ago—or 20, or 40, or 60, or 70, or 80, or 90. They're less helpful, that is, because unless there happen to be three or four other guys in the lineup who get on just as regularly, their contribution is merely to forestall the inevitable. Runs happen, increasingly, when a sudden bang happens, and that means attacking early in the count—because pitchers are sure as hell doing that.

In a league making contact on barely 75 percent of its swings, and a league in which an increasing number of pitchers can throw multiple off-speed pitches for strikes in any count, the only way to consistently generate offense is going to be aggressive. This isn't necessarily true for individuals, like Mookie Betts and Jose Ramirez, who make a lot of contact and have excellent plate discipline, and whose power comes from such natural quickness in a short stroke. Most players have to make tradeoffs, though, whether it be lowering their contact rate or raising their chase rate, in order to consistently make the quality of contact necessary to survive in today's game.

Highest %	Lowest %
Javier Baez – 48.3	Joe Mauer – 4.6
Freddie Freeman – 47.1	Mookie Betts – 9.7
Ozzie Albies – 46.3	Brett Gardner – 10.7
Jose Altuve – 44.2	Jose Ramirez – 12.0
Nick Castellanos – 44.1	Jason Kipnis – 13.8
Joey Gallo – 42.3	Jesus Aguilar – 14.5
Corey Dickerson – 40.9	Xander Bogaerts – 15.8
Salvador Perez – 40.8	Brian Dozier – 16.3
Eddie Rosario – 40.7	Mike Trout – 17.6
Nick Ahmed – 40.4	Yasmani Grandal – 17.6

Top 10 and Bottom 10 Hitters, First-Pitch Swing Rate (2018)

The question isn't which of these lists one prefers, but what they each convey, qualitatively, about the cat-and-mouse game of early-count hitting. Those top five on the left, especially, drive home the fact that for most players, getting aggressive early in the count is now key to keeping strikeout rate down and hitting for power.

For now, the message is: pitchers are coming right after batters with the nastiest stuff they've ever had. Batters had better stop giving away strike one and force hurlers to adjust, or the global OBP crisis is only going to get worse.

—*Matthew Trueblood is an author of Baseball Prospectus.*

A Hymn for the Index Stat

Patrick Dubuque

We survived without computers. I know this, because I remember the day when my dad hooked up his brand-new Atari 400 computer to the back of our 12-inch Magnavox television, and the perfect blue of the memo pad lit up for the first time. I was born just on the edge of that transitional generation, of learning cursive and balancing checkbooks and just doing math all the time, constant manual arithmetic.

It still amazes me. We learned how to sail ships without computers. We learned how to do calculus. We built towers that didn't fall down, most of the time. We engineered catapults to knock them down anyway. We built a robust system of philosophy called "utilitarianism," founded on the principle that the good of an action is evaluated by summing the effects of that action, which is the kind of formula that would make the world's mainframes crash. The whole foundation of statistics as a field is "here's math you could easily do but would die of old age first."

The fact of the matter is that there is too much math in the world to do. There are too many things changing, and too many things too small to notice, for us to handle. At some point, they become too much for the computers to handle as well, which is why we have chaos theory and undetectable earthquakes, but it's not an even fight. At some point, we fall back on intuition, and given how under-equipped we are, we're forced to bestow that intuition with some sort of supernatural superiority, the "gut feeling," that we can't prove because we can only intuit that our intuition is better.

We're all lousy at intuition, and wonderful at lying to ourselves about it. The honest truth is that computers are far better at intuition than we are, because in order to know what feels "off" you have to know what's "on." In order to do that you have to constantly reassess the average of everything, then re-rank your own experience against it.

Test your own, by comparing these three anonymous lines:

Player	G	HR	AVG	OBP	SLG
Player A	156	38	.259	.342	.535
Player B	154	38	.280	.348	.527
Player C	158	38	.266	.343	.509

These all seem like pretty similar players, right? The second one a touch more batted-ball dependent, the third a little less strong, but all pretty good hitters. And you'd be right, about the latter. Not the former.

Here's the breakdown:

- Player A: 1991 Howard Johnson, 141 DRC+
- Player B: 1996 Dean Palmer, 121 DRC+
- Player C: 2018 Giancarlo Stanton, 114 DRC+

Baseball is fortunate to have escaped the seismic shifts of so many other sports, where the talents and performances of other eras are nearly unrecognizable. (And not just other sports: try to explain the greatness of the movie Duck Soup without adjusting for era.) But they're still there, and they're nearly impossible to account for manually, without having to resort to sweeping generalizations like "steroid era" or juiced-ball era" to throw out entire swathes of production.

This is all to say that we should celebrate the index stat, that simple 100-based scale with such a humble aim: just to give context. It's hard to imagine how we lived without them for so long. Sabermetricians have always tried to make their stats look like other stats: True Average mapped to batting average, FIP molded to look like and compare to ERA. It's easy to understand the motivation—these statistics carry an emotional value in them that is hard to resist, as with the .300 hitter and the 2.00 ERA—but even they fall prey to the same loss of scale as their unadjusted counterparts. If a .300 average means different things in different years, does that hold true for a .300 True Average?

Instead, 100 doesn't say anything, except above average or below. And it does it instantly, for every season in every run environment for any statistic we want it to. We should have more index stats: K%+, so we can stop comparing Mike Clevinger's career 9.46 K/9 to Nolan Ryan's 9.55. HBP%+, so we can note that Ron Hunt was getting plunked when nobody else was getting plunked, as opposed to that imitator Brandon Guyer. Some might note how stale these references are and accuse league-adjustment as a backward-looking drive, and this is true. But we're always looking backward, always comparing the new with the expectations already set. The index stat just forces us to be honest.

There's always resistance to a new statistic, especially one so outwardly simple and so internally complex. We tend to stick with what we know, even in the case of formulas that are supposed to tell us what we know. But if your resistance is that it seems too complicated, too counterintuitive, too "black boxy," I encourage you to consider why you feel that way. Because the real world is infinitely more complicated than baseball, where all the pitches go in one basic direction and the baserunners are only allowed to travel in four directions. Baseball statistics based on mixed methodology are almost impossibly intricate. So are skyscrapers and automobiles. That's why we have computers—to take the guesswork out of them.

—*Patrick Dubuque is an author of Baseball Prospectus.*

Index of Names

Agrazal, Dario 100
Archer, Chris 48
Ashcraft, Braxton 94, 112
Barrett, Jake 100
Bell, Josh 22
Brault, Steven 50
Brubaker, J.T. 100
Burdi, Nick 100
Cabrera, Melky 24
Castro, Rodolfo 111
Cervelli, Francisco 26
Chisenhall, Lonnie 82
Craig, Will 83, 111
Crick, Kyle 52
Cruz, Oneil 84, 105
Davis, Jonah 98
Diaz, Elias 28
Dickerson, Corey 30
Escobar, Luis 95, 110
Feliz, Michael 54
Franklin, Nick 98
Frazier, Adam 32
Gomez, Roberto 100
Gonzalez, Erik 34
Hayes, Ke'Bryan 85, 104
Holmes, Clay 56
Jennings, Steven 96
Kang, Jung-ho 86
Kela, Keone 58
Keller, Mitch 97, 103
Kingham, Nick 60
Kivlehan, Patrick 98
Kramer, Kevin 87, 108
Kuhl, Chad 62
Liranzo, Jesus 100
Liriano, Francisco 64
Lyles, Jordan 66
Lyons, Tyler 100
MacGregor, Travis 98, 112
Marte, Starling 36
Martin, Jason 88, 108
Maurer, Brandon 68
McRae, Alex 100
Mitchell, Calvin 89, 106
Moran, Colin 38
Musgrove, Joe 70
Neverauskas, Dovydas 100
Newman, Kevin 40, 109
Ogle, Braeden 100, 112
Osuna, Jose 42
Polanco, Gregory 44
Reyes, Pablo 46
Reynolds, Bryan 90, 109
Rodriguez, Richard 72
Sanchez, Lolo 91, 110
Santana, Edgar 74
Slegers, Aaron 100
Stallings, Jacob 98
Swaggerty, Travis 92, 104
Taillon, Jameson 76
Thomas, Tahnaj 110
Tucker, Cole 93, 107

Uselton, Conner 98
Vazquez, Felipe 78
Williams, Trevor 80

Ballpark diagrams for Baseball Prospectus are created by THIRTY81Project, a design concept offering original ballpark artwork, including the new 'Ballparks of 2019' 11 x 17 color print.

Visit **www.thirty81project.com** for full details.

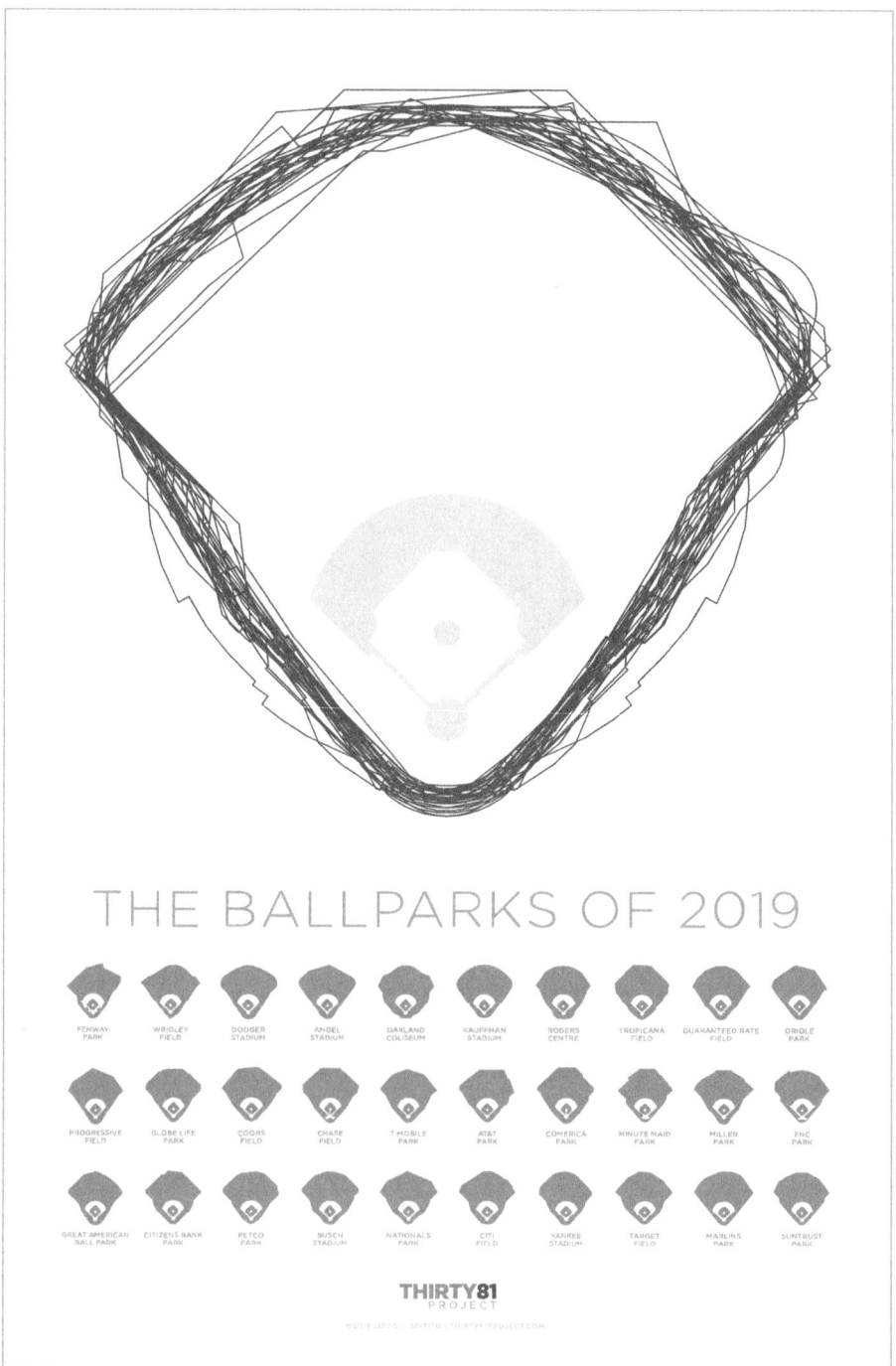